GOD vs. RELIGION

Books by Dr. Creflo Dollar

In the Presence of God

Live Without Fear

Not Guilty

Love, Live, and Enjoy Life

Breaking Out of Trouble

Walking in the Confidence of God in Troubled Times

Claim Your Victory Today

8 Steps to Create the Life You Want

Winning in Troubled Times

The Holy Spirit, Your Financial Advisor

Real Manhood

You're Supposed to Be Wealthy

GOD vs. RELIGION

10 Reasons to Break Free from the Bondage of Religious Tradition

DR. CREFLO DOLLAR

FaithWords

NEW YORK   BOSTON   NASHVILLE

FaithWords
Hachette Book Group
1290 Avenue of the Americas, New York, NY 10104
faithwords.com
twitter.com/faithwords

This book was originally published in hardcover as
Why I Hate Religion by FaithWords.

First trade paperback edition: September 2016

FaithWords is a division of Hachette Book Group, Inc. The FaithWords name and logo are trademarks of Hachette Book Group, Inc.

The publisher is not responsible for websites (or their content) that are not owned by the publisher.

The Hachette Speakers Bureau provides a wide range of authors for speaking events. To find out more, go to www.hachettespeakersbureau.com or call (866) 376-6591.

The Library of Congress has catalogued the hardcover edition
Why I Hate Religion as follows:

Dollar, Creflo A.
  Why I hate religion : 10 reasons to break free from the bondage of religious tradition / Dr. Creflo Dollar.—First [edition].
    pages cm
  ISBN 978-1-4555-7729-3 (hardcover)—ISBN 978-1-4789-5960-1 (audio cd)—ISBN 978-1-4789-5961-8 (audio download)—ISBN 978-1-4555-7730-9 (ebook)
  1. Apologetics. 2. Christianity—Essence, genius, nature. 3. Tradition (Theology) 4. Religion—Controversial literature. I. Title.
  BT1103.D65 2015
  239—dc23

                                                                        2015023588

ISBN: 978-1-4555-7732-3 (pbk.)

Printed in the United States of America

RRD C

10 9 8 7 6 5 4 3 2 1

CONTENTS

Woe to you, scribes and Pharisees, hypocrites! for ye are like unto whited sepulchers, which indeed appear beautiful outward, but are within full of dead *men's* bones, and of all <u>uncleanness</u>. Even so ye also outwardly appear righteous unto men, but within ye are full of hypocrisy and iniquity.

MATTHEW 23:27–28

<u>uncleaness</u> : (G167)
in a moral sense: the impurity
of lustful, luxurious, profligate
living; of impure motives.
profligate: wildly extravagant spending.
extravagant, high Rolling, spendthrift,
squandering, thriftless, unthrifty, wasteful.

INTRODUCTION

I hate religion! That's right. I'm a preacher, and I said it myself. Why? Because "religion" portrays the image of what it defines as godliness but has no power to back it up. It thrives on the concept of attaining right standing with God through self-effort while downplaying what Jesus has done for us. Unfortunately, religion has caused many people to actually turn away from God and the promises contained in the Bible. A concentration on religion has been responsible for death, destruction, and strife among people of all ethnicities and backgrounds. It is why denominations cannot get along, and it is what provokes extremists to carry out suicide missions in the name of God. Religion is the counterfeit of having a real relationship with the Lord.

Now, let me make another bold statement: God hates religion, too! Jesus used every opportunity to blast the religious leaders of His day for carrying out vain traditions that meant nothing. Just read Matthew 23, where Jesus rebuked the Pharisees for saying one thing but doing another and for following blindly after rituals and Law-based traditions done only to make them look good.

Religion is made up of man's ideas, interpretations, and prejudices based on selfish desires, attempts to control others, and a stubborn determination to be right. Where is God in that? Religion completely takes God out of the equation and replaces Him with the god of "self" in the form of self-effort, self-righteousness, and self-gratification. *True* Christianity is not a religion; it is a *relationship* with Christ. Now, *that* I love!

> **T**rue *Christianity is not a religion; it is a* **relationship** *with Christ.*

In this book, we will explore what religious tradition teaches *about* God versus what a relationship *with* God is all about. I will give you my top ten reasons why I hate religion and show you how religion actually hinders your relationship with God. I may step on your traditions, I may contradict what you've been told all your life, I might even make you angry; but just stick with me until the end. After I present the difference between religion and a real relationship with God, I believe you will see things in a different light. You may even find you hate religion, too!

Now, more than ever before, people need to hear the truth about the gospel of Jesus Christ. It is a message of hope, not condemnation; liberty, not religious bondage; grace, not self-effort. Most of the things we have grown up hearing about God are completely incorrect! We have come to relate to God as an angry taskmaster who is waiting for us to mess up so He can strike us down with a lightning bolt. We have gotten so far away from what Christianity is really about and have presented a picture of God that actually turns people away from wanting to know Him. It is time for us to get back to the simplicity of the Gospel and share the truth about the love and grace of God with the world.

It is time for us to get back to the simplicity of the Gospel and share the truth about the love and grace of God with the world.

When I reflect on my own life, my journey as a Christian, and my understanding of the Word of God, I thank God for continuing to enlighten my understanding on this topic. There are religious ideas that I grew up with that I have come to find out are simply flat-out wrong. My hope is that you carefully look at the religious misconceptions that you have heard and internalized and discover the truth about what it means to have a real relationship with Jesus Christ. It is through relationship, not religion, that we are empowered to do the works that Jesus did and more. Join me on this journey as I share with you why I hate religion.

GOD vs.
RELIGION

The love of money is the root of all evil, which
while some coveted after, they have erred from
the faith, and pierced themselves through with
many sorrows.

I TIMOTHY 6:10

Let them shout for joy, and be glad, that favour
my righteous cause; yea, let them say continually,
Let the Lord be magnified, which hath pleasure
in the prosperity of his servant.

PSALM 35:27

Will a man rob God? Yet ye have robbed me. But
ye say, Wherein have we robbed thee? In titles
and offerings.

MALACHI 3:8

REASON #10: RELIGION TEACHES THAT MONEY IS THE ROOT OF ALL EVIL

Visit any barbershop or beauty parlor on a Saturday morning and you will see people from all walks of life discussing any number of topics. You'll hear the latest gossip as well as everything from politics and sports to finances and religion. Religion and money always seem to be the hot topics. Saved or unsaved, almost everyone has heard the saying "Money is the root of all evil." This phrase has shaped the mind-sets of millions and has kept them in financial bondage.

The notion that money is the root of all evil comes from 1 Timothy 6:10, which says, "For the love of money is the root of all evil." This is one of the most misquoted verses in the Bible. I've heard preacher after preacher use this Scripture as their basis to support the teaching that Christians should be broke or that money shouldn't be talked about in the church. This erroneous teaching has kept many people in financial bondage and has caused them to live under the burden of lack and debt.

These preachers teach their congregations that God uses poverty to humble them. They tell them to be content with what they have because money is evil, and it will ruin them. I've even heard statements such as, "It's godly to be poor" and "It's not God's will for His people to prosper." These false doctrines have been passed down through the generations. It's no wonder that people are wary of ministers who preach the true Gospel where prosperity is concerned.

Most people think that prosperity is money. While that is not incorrect, it is incomplete. Biblical prosperity encompasses every area of your life. This includes your mind, will, and emotions, as well as your physical body. It also includes your marriage, family, business, and finances.

Biblical prosperity encompasses every area
of your life.

Third John 2:2 says, "Beloved, I wish above all things that thou mayest prosper and be in health, even as thy soul prospereth." Like any father, God wants you to have well-being in every area of your life, including your finances. Religion has trained you to think that it's okay to have success in other areas of your life, as long as you're broke. The sad thing is that many people have bought this lie.

Many people are okay with hearing sermons on salvation or on renewing their minds, but they don't want the minister to preach about money. What confounds me is that the problem most people have is money—or the lack of it. The majority of church folks are broke, busted, disgusted, and up to their eyeballs in debt.

Jesus said, "The Spirit of the Lord [is] upon Me, because He has anointed Me [the Anointed One, the Messiah] to preach the good news (the Gospel) to the poor" (Luke 4:18 AMP). What is the good news to the poor? It's that they don't have to be poor anymore! And the only way to be delivered from poverty is through hearing the Word of God on prosperity and then doing what it says.

Religion teaches that although we should trust God in all other areas of our life, money is something we need to handle ourselves. Well, we all know our own track record of handling money, and for some of us it's not so good. To us, money is a big deal; but to God, it's a small detail. He wants us to prosper financially, but His Word says to trust Him enough to loosen our death grip on it.

> *To us, money is a big deal; but to God, it's a small detail. He wants us to prosper financially, but His Word says to trust Him enough to loosen our death grip on it.*

"He that is faithful in that which is least is faithful also in much: and he that is unjust in the least is unjust also in much" (Luke 16:10). Money is the least important way we show our trust in Him. When we can demonstrate to ourselves that we can trust God enough to give monetarily, we'll know that we can trust Him for the really big things, such as peace, joy, abundance, prosperity, and all of the other promises He's made to us.

We get so fearful of the shysters of the world hiding out in the pulpit and posing as honest ministers, that when we get to the point in church when we hear it's time for the offering, we freeze up. We think, "There's no way I'm giving anything to this guy and let him line his pockets with my money." Did you catch that? "*My* money!"

Child of God, everything is the Lord's, including money. He

doesn't need yours! But He does need your trust, and when you give because you want to, instead of out of a sense of duty or obligation, it opens up the floodgates of blessings He wants to pour out on you. "But this I say, He which soweth sparingly shall reap also sparingly; and he which soweth bountifully shall reap also bountifully. Every man according as he purposeth in his heart, so let him give; not grudgingly, or of necessity: for God loveth a cheerful giver" (2 Cor. 9:6–7).

Is Money Evil?

I want you to look at 1 Timothy 6:10 and read it more closely this time: "For the love of money is the root of all evil." Nowhere in this Scripture does it say that money in and of itself is the root of all evil. Many have taught this Scripture to mean something entirely different from what God said. The *love* of money, or having a wrong relationship with it, is the root of all evil. That one word—love—makes a huge difference.

> *Nowhere in this Scripture does it say that money in and of itself is the root of all evil.*

Let's say that I placed a one-hundred-dollar bill on a table. Is that money good or bad? Neither. What makes money good or bad depends on who holds it. If the money belongs to someone who tithes and sows money to advance the kingdom of God, then it is good. On the other hand, if you put the same money into the hands of a terrorist, who uses the money to kill people, then it becomes bad. Is the money bad in and of itself? No. Whoever has the money determines the outcome of that money.

Having a wrong relationship with money means that you trust money and material possessions more than you trust God. Using things to try to answer spiritual problems is an indication of having a wrong relationship with money. I'm sure you know someone who shops when he or she is depressed. Instead of turning to God as his or her Source, this person tries to find comfort in things. God is the answer to any adversity, not possessions. God doesn't have a problem with your having money; He just doesn't want money to have you.

> *God doesn't have a problem with your having money;*
> *He just doesn't want money to have you.*

Having a right relationship with money means we see it for what it is—a tool. God sends it our way in generous proportions when we seek Him first, and it's one of the ways He can bless us so much that it overflows into someone else's life. One of the ways we can gauge if we have the right attitude about money is if we give to express our gratitude for what Jesus did for us, and if it's done out of love. If it's not, no preacher in the world can make it right. "And if I give all my possessions to feed the poor, and if I surrender my body to be burned, but do not have love, it profits me nothing" (1 Cor. 13:3 NASB).

The Truth About Money

Money is an amplifier. There are several lottery winners who have spent their entire fortune in a few short years. They've gone from poor to rich to poor again. Instead of using their money wisely, they have used it foolishly to satisfy their desires. They continued to live the same hellish lifestyle they lived before they became wealthy. They just had a lot more money at their disposal. Money didn't cause their misfortune; they did it to themselves.

Proverbs 1:32 says, "The prosperity of fools shall destroy them." If you put a million dollars in the hands of a fool, he will spend it frivolously. Because this person lacks knowledge and a relationship with God, money only amplifies his destructive lifestyle. Just think of the rock stars or movie stars who rose from obscurity only to die young from a drug overdose. You are the one who determines what kind of relationship you will have with money—good or bad.

> *You are the one who determines what kind of relationship you will have with money—good or bad.*

If your heart and your spirit aren't right, no amount of money will make them right. Trying to chase down money and snatch up some of it for yourself is trusting in your own abilities, instead of having faith that God wants to be your financial Source. It's a great example of living according to the Law instead of by faith in His favor.

"For as many as are of the works of the law are under the curse: for it is written, 'Cursed is every one that continueth not in all things which are written in the book of the law to do them.' But that no man is justified by the law in the sight of God, it is evident: for, the just shall live by faith. And the law is not of faith: but, the man that doeth them shall live in them" (Gal. 3:10–12). It's about whether you put your faith in what God's own Son did for us more than two thousand years ago, or in a pile of money.

The right type of relationship with money is one that honors

God. Proverbs 3:9–10 says, "Honour the LORD with thy substance, and with the firstfruits of all thine increase: So shall thy barns be filled with plenty, and thy presses shall burst out with new wine." You honor God by trusting Him as your Source, not money! Your trust will cause your account to overflow with more than enough.

God wants His people to prosper. Psalm 35:27 says, "Let them shout for joy, and be glad, that favour my righteous cause: yea, let them say continually, Let the Lord be magnified, which hath pleasure in the prosperity of his servant." When a Christian says that having money is not of God, this person is not walking in the Spirit because that kind of thinking does not line up with the Scriptures.

Agreeing with God

We know that *walking in the Spirit* is defined as "being in agreement with God's Word." That means that whatever God says is right, you say is right, and whatever He says is wrong, you say is wrong. Sounds simple enough, right? Yet many people have a problem agreeing with God when it comes to money. They believe they can be healed because of Isaiah 53:5, but these same people have trouble saying, "I'm prosperous," even though prosperity is also in the Bible. When believers say they are rich, they aren't being arrogant; they're simply agreeing with the Word of God.

God has *already* blessed you with all spiritual blessings in heavenly places (see Eph. 1:3). All of the promises of God are available to you if you line yourself up with the Word. It's your job to find out what the Word says, and then to live by it, including the area of financial stewardship.

*All of the promises of God are available
to you if you line yourself up with the Word.*

One way to gain access to the financial blessings that are found
in the Bible is to begin tithing, or giving 10 percent of your *gross*
income to the Lord as well as giving offerings. Malachi 3:10 says,
"Bring all the tithes (the whole tenth of your income) into the
storehouse, that there may be food in My house, and prove Me
now by it, says the Lord of hosts, if I will not open the windows
of heaven for you and pour you out a blessing, that there shall
not be room enough to receive it" (AMP).

If we trust in God for our prosperity, He promises to deliver
in a big way. In the Old Testament, after Abram slew all his enemies, he gave his tithe to God to praise and thank Him for the
victory. He refused to take any wealth from the king, lest anyone
should say the king was his source and not God (see Gen. 14:20,
23). God honored Abram's offering by declaring He was Abram's
reward, and then blessing him with the son he had always wanted
(see Gen. 15:1–4).

The principle of seedtime and harvest will work for anyone
who gets involved with it. When our giving is based on our love
for God and our desire to honor Him with our increase, He will
honor us. Tithing and financial giving are acts of love that flow
from an appreciation for what God has done in our lives. God
will always respond when we do things from a position of love
and obedience. When God says that He will "pour out a blessing" on you, He's not talking about a car or a house. *Blessing*
means "empowered to prosper; empowered to have success." God
promises to give you the ability to obtain wealth. He wants to
empower you to do things that you couldn't do before. He does

this by putting His "super" abilities on your natural abilities to produce supernatural results in *every* area of your life, including your finances.

> *When our giving is based on our love for God*
> *and our desire to honor Him with our increase,*
> *He will honor us.*

I have discovered that tithing allows you to hear from God more clearly about what you need to do to prosper in your specific situation. God knows a million ways to get you out of debt and into abundant living, but all you need is one. He will give you business ideas, witty inventions, wisdom, and step-by-step instructions on how to prosper, as well as insight, concepts, and ideas that will bring you into wealth. The key is that you obey Him and follow the Holy Spirit's guidance. God wants to help you and be there to meet your needs. He says, "Call to Me and I will answer you and show you great and mighty things, fenced in and hidden, which you do not know (do not distinguish and recognize, have knowledge of and understand)" (Jer. 33:3 AMP).

> *God wants to help you and be there to meet*
> *your needs.*

Another way to gain access to financial blessings is to realize that by grace you are blessed financially through faith and trust in the finished works of Jesus Christ. Financial blessings should not be your goal. Seeking God should be your goal. Then, the financial blessing becomes a by-product of seeking God. Matthew 6:33 says, "But seek ye first the kingdom of God, and His righteousness; and all these things shall be added unto you." It would be an act of perversion for you to seek things when the system was designed for things to seek you! When God is your Source, you have access to all of His resources. Who wants the golden eggs when you can have the golden goose?

What Are You Hiding?

I remember when the Lord first told me to minister on prosperity. I knew that religious demons would fight me tooth and nail to try to stop me from bringing understanding on this subject to the Body of Christ. I've been branded for this assignment. What preacher in his right mind, with a last name like Dollar, would preach about money unless God called him to do it?

I know that what God says about prosperity is true. I live it daily. I tithe and give offerings because I love God and want to bless others. Not surprisingly, money finds its way to me. God has prospered me greatly for trusting Him as my Source. Some people have criticized me because of the prosperity God has blessed me with, but I refuse to be a preacher who knows about prosperity and doesn't teach others how to obtain it from a biblical perspective. God is not a broke God, so why would He want His children to be broke? He owns the cattle on a thousand hills, and He owns the hills as well (see Ps. 50:10). He has prospered me, and He wants to prosper you. *Amen!*

Prosperity is a message that Satan doesn't want you to hear, and he uses religion to try to discourage believers from even having faith in God to prosper them. Now that you know the truth, the devil will try to get you to doubt God's Word (see Mark 4:15). His most powerful weapon is suggestion. He will try to get you to step out of agreement with God, because he knows it can stop your blessings from manifesting.

> *Prosperity is a message that Satan doesn't want you to hear, and he uses religion to try to discourage believers from even having faith in God to prosper them.*

No doubt many of you have heard the "hellfire and damnation" speech a lot of religious leaders feed their congregation about being cursed for not giving enough money in the offering plate. They quote a Scripture out of context, twist it around, and try to use it to pressure people to give out of guilt. A favorite one is from the book of Malachi: "Will a man rob God? Yet ye have robbed me. But ye say, 'Wherein have we robbed thee?' In tithes and offerings. Ye are cursed with a curse: for ye have robbed me, even this whole nation" (Mal. 3:8–9).

What they conveniently leave out is the heart of the matter. Reading on, we learn that God promises to bless us, not curse us, when we believe Him enough to give as He instructs us to (see Mal. 3:10–12). When religion deceives us and pulls this trick on us, it's no wonder we have trouble trusting!

When somebody tells you that it's God's will for you to be poor, don't align yourself with these words or this way of thinking. If you do, you'll once again lean on the arm of the flesh and open yourself up to an attack from the enemy. Jeremiah 17:5 says, "Thus saith the Lord; 'Cursed be the man that trusteth in man, and maketh flesh his arm, and whose heart departeth from the Lord.'" A curse is "an empowerment to fail," and you don't want failure to manifest in any area of your life.

The sad thing is that a lot of these people actually believe it's God's intent for them to be busted and broke! This line of reasoning is of the flesh, not of the Spirit (see 1 Cor. 2:14). A check of the Scriptures shows that not only is this untrue, but God's plan is for over-the-top abundance for us (see 2 Cor. 9:8).

One other thing: When we give from the heart and in the right spirit, to bless others, we won't have to be anxious or worried about whether the money will vanish and never reappear. We won't need to concern ourselves with working extra hard to make up for the money that left our checking account. God's got this, and He'll return it to us greatly multiplied (see Luke 6:38).

Learn to stick with what the Word says. Everything you need—all blessings, healing, deliverance, abundance, and protection—begins with trusting God as the Source for everything. But when you ignore the Word, or refuse to find out what it says, you are guaranteed to remain in your problems. However, when you agree with God's Word on prosperity and trust Him more than you trust money as your source, look out. Supernatural abundance and profit are sure to come your way! Money is *not* the root of all evil. It's what you do with it that counts.

Everything you need—all blessings, healing, deliverance, abundance, and protection—begins with trusting God as the Source for everything.

For even when we were with you, this we
commanded you, that if any would not work,
neither should he eat.

II THESSALONIANS 3:10

There is a way which seemeth right unto a man,
but the end thereof *are* the ways of death.

PROVERBS 14:12

And we know that all things work together for
good to them that love God, to them who are
the called according to *his* purpose.

ROMANS 8:28

REASON #9: RELIGION BLAMES PROBLEMS ON THE SOVEREIGNTY OF GOD

I often say that excuses are nails used to build houses of failure. Some Christians come up with one excuse after another for why the Word doesn't work for them. If they don't receive an immediate answer after praying, they are quick to give up and say, "Well, God is in control," or "It must be God's will for me to go through this." The truth is that this type of thinking is fleshly. God does not want you to suffer; He wants you receive a breakthrough. Many people don't realize that there are other reasons why their prayers are not answered.

What holds most Christians back from receiving the things they are asking God for is a religious mind-set that blames Him for their problems rather than focusing on the true culprit—themselves. Instead of looking at the part they play in a situation, they shift the blame and accept a life of sickness, poverty, and defeat, and they use religion to try to justify it.

People often fail to examine what they are *not* doing in their lives. They don't read their Bibles or apply what they read to their

daily lives. Yet they don't understand why things just don't seem
to be working out. Religion has taught them that God decides
whether or not they will receive answers. The "sovereignty" of
God has become their excuse for not seeing results. *Easton's Bible
Dictionary* defines the *sovereignty of God* as "God's absolute right
to do all things according to His own good pleasure." Basically,
this definition says that God chooses to do what He wants to
do. If He doesn't *feel* like answering your prayers or if you have
done something to anger Him, then He won't; but if He is in a
good mood, He just *might* give you what you want. This is religion's answer to why someone's prayer goes unanswered. This
type of thinking, however, is contrary to the Word and completely
negates the fact that our good works have nothing to do with God
being good to us. Neither is God playing a game of "eeny, meeny,
miny, moe" to decide whose prayers He will answer and whose
He won't.

Lazy Christians

Mark 11:24 says, "Therefore I say unto you, What things soever
ye desire, when ye pray, believe that ye receive them, and ye shall
have them." The key to answered prayer is believing that you have
the answer when you pray, because the answer has already been
provided by grace and through your faith you have received it.
This is a perfect picture of resting in the finished works of Jesus.
Resting in God or the finished works of Jesus does not mean inactivity. You rest while you work, knowing with confidence that it is
already provided and taken care of. To rest in God is the highest
kind of faith. When you pray, you rest in the finished works of
Jesus for the answers to your prayers.

*Resting in God or the finished works of Jesus
does not mean inactivity.*

As Christians, we must not use resting in God as an excuse for laziness. Unfortunately, too many people in the Body of Christ only want to say "Abracadabra" and have money suddenly appear out of thin air. Sadly, they are deceived and misinformed. They think they can sit at home and wait for God to bless them. It doesn't work that way. Money doesn't fall from the sky.

When it comes to seeing financial increase, there is a role that honest labor plays in that process. God expects you to work. This is clearly spelled out in 2 Thessalonians 3:10: "If any would not work, neither should he eat." Laziness and not resting in God while you work disqualify you from receiving a harvest, and limits God from moving on your behalf. Listen to the fate of the lazy man in Proverbs 24:30–31: "I went by the field of the lazy man, and by the vineyard of the man void of understanding; And, behold, it was all grown over with thorns, and nettles were covering its face, and its stone wall was broken down" (AMP). Even though this man was able to work, his laziness caused his vineyard not to produce a harvest. Anyone who refuses to take care of his or her household and uses religious excuses to cover up slothfulness will experience the same thing—a house in shambles.

Only diligent people—those who rest in God's abilities—will reap a harvest, not the people who work only when someone stands over their shoulder or who only do enough work to avoid termination. Proverbs 6:6–8 says, "Go to the ant, thou sluggard; consider her ways, and be wise: Which having no guide, overseer, or ruler, provideth her meat in the summer, and gathereth her food in the harvest." The ant can be admired for its work ethic. No one tells the ant what to do. It is responsible, diligent, and hard-working. However, if we don't rest, then God won't work, but if we rest, then God works. We can't afford to be working and God resting. Let's rest while He works!

> *Only diligent people—those who rest in God's abilities—will reap a harvest.*

Some people don't want to look through the classified ads or go from business to business to fill out applications. They want to sit at home and "trust God only." Although they keep checking their mailboxes for unexpected income, they only receive bills. They then try the lottery but only become discouraged when some-one else wins. They fail to realize that they are in this situation because they are not doing what needs to be done in the natural realm, and trusting God while they do it!

When things don't quickly change, they lose hope. Proverbs 13:12 states that not having your hopes fulfilled will make your heart sick. That's why many people fall into depression and despair. Proverbs 21:25 says, "The desire of the slothful killeth him; for his hands refuse to labour." Nothing moves God like a believer who decides to step out in faith. But if you don't do your part and work, you won't see results. Once you begin to do something, however, God is able to bless the work of your hands because you understand how to rest while you work.

A young man once told me that he couldn't do any manual labor because he didn't want anything to happen to his hands. He needed to preserve them because he was an artist. Instead of working, he sat at home while his wife struggled to make enough money to pay the bills and take care of their children. That's not biblical, that's foolishness!

God can't bring a harvest to a lazy person who won't work and trust Him. If you want a breakthrough in your life, you must learn the power of trusting and resting in God. Wealth never comes into the hands of a lazy person or the person who uses religion to try to magically get something to happen. Proverbs 10:4 says, "He becomes poor who works with a slack and idle hand, but the hand of the diligent makes rich" (AMP). I believe you must be diligent in rest while you work.

> *If you want a breakthrough in your life, you must learn the power of trusting and resting in God.*

Work the Word

Along with the work that you must do in this physical world, you also have to work the Word. If you want the promises of God to come to pass in your life, you must know what the Bible says regarding your situation and how to apply the Word to your life, not just religiously quote Scriptures. There are people who can recite the Bible from cover to cover, but they don't have a personal relationship with Jesus. Therefore, they still experience lack in their lives.

Working the Word means that you read and study your Bible and then receive a revelation of what the Word means. It involves the process of meditation as well, which means to ponder the Word and turn it over in your mind. God sent the Holy Spirit to help you receive a better understanding of the Scripture. He is your Comforter, Helper, Counselor, Advocate,

Intercessor, Strengthener, and Standby (see John 14:16 AMP). He was deposited into your heart the day you accepted Christ (see Rom. 5:5). Although everyone has access to the wisdom of the Holy Spirit, you have to learn how to have Him operate on your behalf.

> *Working the Word means that you read and study your Bible and then receive a revelation of what the Word means.*

The Holy Spirit wants to move in your life, but He is unable to do anything until you trust Him, open your mouth, and speak Word-based directions. He cannot do anything if the Word is not operating in you. When you don't spend time reading your Bible and getting the Word in your heart, you limit what the Holy Spirit is able to do. He can only bring to pass the Word that you trust, know, and declare. If you don't know what God has promised you, the Holy Spirit doesn't have anything to work with. Remember, He's a helper. It's up to you to find out what rightfully belongs to you.

How much of the Word do you have operating on the inside of you? In other words, are you a doer of the Word rather than a hearer only? It's not enough to be able to quote the Word. You have to *rely* on the Word with confidence. It needs to be the basis by which you conduct and govern your life. This goes beyond head-knowledge of the Word to what I call "heart-knowledge."

Heart-knowledge occurs when you become so intimate with God that you begin to hear the voice behind what you read in the Bible or hear from the pulpit. God has given you the *logos* Word, or the "written Word." The prerequisite to hearing His voice is knowing the written Word. When the Holy Spirit speaks to you, or reveals the written Word to you, you have received the *rhema* Word from God.

> *Heart-knowledge occurs when you become so intimate with God that you begin to hear the voice behind what you read in the Bible or hear from the pulpit.*

The *rhema* Word is the prophetic Word that God gives you to strengthen you and reveal, or give insight into, God's supernatural plan for a situation. It's inside knowledge that will help you overcome anything. God desires to speak to all of us. He has something to say about every situation in your life. Unfortunately, if there's no Word in your heart, He is limited in what He can say to you through the *rhema* Word.

Can you see why you must become a student of the Word? Think about it. If God has the answer to every one of your problems and all you need is to have the Word working in your life, wouldn't you take the time to study it? There are people, however, who would rather toss the blame on God's sovereignty than to take the time to get in the Word. They don't want to work at trusting God to bring the Word to pass in their lives.

Knowing Your Covenant

When you hear people talk about the sovereignty of God, realize that they are strangers to what the Bible says and to their covenant (see Eph. 2:12). Because of the covenant, the promises that God made to mankind thousands of years ago still hold true today.

If they knew the Word, they would know what God says about working and blessings.

A covenant is a vow, a promise, or a pledge between two or more parties to carry out the terms of an agreement. A covenant during biblical times was stronger than any contract that you sign today—it was a matter of life and death. Covenants at that time were sealed with blood and couldn't be broken except by death. We have a blood covenant with God through Jesus' death and the shedding of His blood. This covenant guarantees us victory in life (see Heb. 12:24). The terms and conditions of the covenant are found in the Bible, but religion has taught people to carry their Bibles to church on Sunday and leave them in the car until they return the following week.

Your Bible should not lie on your coffee table or the backseat of your car without ever being read. It is the key to having wholeness in every area of your life. Unfortunately, many people never take the time to find out what it says. Instead of gaining strength from the Word, they throw their hands up in the air and say, "Well, you know God is God. If it was meant for me to have it, He would have done something by now." They don't know their rights because they never take the time to find out what they are.

Even though God is sovereign, He can't do whatever He wants because He is bound by the Word. If He promised to prosper those who seek Him first, then He is bound by His promise. If He didn't do what He said, then He would be a liar. And we know that He can never lie. "God is not a man, that he should lie; neither the son of man, that he should repent: hath he said, and shall he not do it? or hath he spoken, and shall he not make it good?" (Num. 23:19). Once God has spoken, it will come to pass (see Titus 1:2). God says in Psalm 89:34, "My covenant will I not break, nor alter the thing that is gone out of my lips."

God will never change His mind about what He has said.

All He needs you to do is put Him in remembrance of His Word (see Isa. 43:26). That is why it is important for you to be a student of the Word and not just a religious churchgoer. Once you find out what the Word promises regarding healing, wealth, deliverance, peace, and so forth, you can have it in your life. Unfortunately, because this takes *faith*, most people don't take the time to do it. They transfer the blame to God when things aren't working right, rather than taking responsibility for their own situation.

> *God will never change His mind about what He has said.*

The Flesh Versus the Word

The main reason people don't get into the Word is because they don't think it takes all that to receive from God. When this is your attitude, you have positioned yourself to oppose the Word and have revealed your true nature—laziness. It is time to recognize when you're operating in the flesh and change your mind-set to line up with the Word. Romans 8:5 says, "For they that are after the flesh do mind the things of the flesh; but they that are after the Spirit the things of the Spirit." The flesh will tell you that you don't need to read your Bible or spend time in prayer. The flesh doesn't care that the Word is a person's connection to God.

Christians who renew their minds with the Word and learn what it says will experience the promises of God. They will tithe and sow seeds to the advancement of the kingdom of God. They will attend church to hear the Word and take the time to study it to hear the voice behind God's written words. These people will diligently spend time getting to know God. Their faith will always be rewarded.

It's time to stop blaming God for the situations in which we find ourselves. God is not the problem; a fleshly mind-set is! Where a person is today is the result of his or her choices, not God's sovereignty. So I encourage you to choose to be diligent and work hard, resting in God as your Source. Do your part spiritually, and in the natural realm, and God will bless your diligence. Proverbs 13:4 says, "The soul of the sluggard desireth, and hath nothing: but the soul of the diligent shall be made fat." Remember, the choices you make determine what you have and where you are in life.

It's time to stop blaming God for the situations in which we find ourselves.

For there is no respect of persons with God.

ROMANS 2:11

Ye have heard that it was said by them of old
time, Thou shalt not commit adultery: but I say
unto you, That whoever looketh on a woman to
lust after her hath committed adultery with her
already in his heart.

MATTHEW 5:27–28

But I say unto you, Love your enemies, bless them
that curse you, do good to them that hate you,
and pray for them which despitefully use you,
and persecute you.

MATTHEW 5:44

REASON #8: RELIGION ALLOWS A JUDGMENTAL ATTITUDE TO DIVIDE THE CHURCH

How many times have you watched Christians turn their noses up at people whom they perceive to be sinners? A perfect example that I have witnessed is when a young man comes to church wearing an oversize football jersey with baggy jeans large enough to fit two people. He's wearing a scarf under a backward-turned baseball cap. Tattoos are visible on his arms, diamond earrings sparkle in both ears, and platinum chains hang around his neck. The first reaction from Christians is shock that anyone dressed like that would dare show up in church. They are quick to call him a heathen and label him as a drug dealer or a gang member. In a lot of people's minds, he is definitely on his way to hell.

The same attitude tends to apply to the young, pregnant single mother who shows up at church or the divorced man who comes to church with another woman. Even though these individuals haven't said a word, many congregation members will pass judgment on them. This is a huge problem among Christians. Unfortunately, religion has taught many believers to judge others without knowing their hearts. This attitude isn't biblical or Godly, and it definitely doesn't reflect the grace and love of God. No one wants to admit that they have a judgmental attitude, but the truth is that many do. People who are not saved, or new born-again Christians, can really become discouraged by Christians who forget about the grace and love that were extended to them by God. We must get rid of the judgmental, self-righteous attitudes that push people away from God. Instead, we must show mercy and compassion toward others by letting them know that God loves them and has empowered them to be overcomers in life.

> We must get rid of the judgmental, self-righteous
> attitudes that push people away from God.

Division in the Church

Jesus warns Christians about the dangers of judging others, yet many of them wear their judgmental attitudes as a badge of honor, not knowing that they will receive the greater condemnation for their actions. Read what He said in Matthew 7:1–2:

> Do not judge and criticize and condemn others, so that you
> may not be judged and criticized and condemned yourselves.
> For just as you judge and criticize and condemn others, you
> will be judged and criticized and condemned, and in accordance with the measure you [use to] deal out to others, it will
> be dealt out again to you. (AMP)

Christians have gotten into the habit of judging their brothers and sisters in the Lord over everything from men wearing their hair too long and women wearing makeup, to not speaking in tongues. These types of issues have caused rifts in the Body of Christ, which ultimately have led to the formation of the denominational churches that are in existence today. Not only that, but these issues cause believers to get into a type of legalism that actually keeps them in bondage instead of setting them free.

A law-based mind-set is focused on doing things through self-effort in order to gain God's approval. As a result, the focus is taken off the finished works of Christ as the criteria for our acceptance by the Father and puts the focus on what people are doing or not doing to determine whether God loves and accepts them. This completely goes against the objective of Jesus coming to the earth and redeeming mankind.

> *A law-based mind-set is focused on doing things through self-effort in order to gain God's approval.*

In Galatians 5:1, the Apostle Paul warned against becoming entangled with legalism as New Testament believers when he said, "Stand fast in the liberty wherewith Christ hath made us free, and be not entangled again with the yoke of bondage." He was talking about the liberty that comes through God's grace being threatened by the legalism of Old Testament laws that some Christians were trying to implement in their lives and in the lives of others, even though they had been set free from the Law and the condemnation that came with it.

The Law (the rules and guidelines God set up for the people of Israel in the Old Testament) was established in order to make people aware of their sin and ultimately show them that they needed a Savior. In the Old Testament, the Israelites had to offer continual animal sacrifices to God in order to atone for their sins.

They worked to keep the Law as best they could, but the reality was that it could not be kept in its entirety. This was not because the Law was not good, but because the fallen nature of man prevented the people from being able to accomplish what they were trying to do through their own efforts. Their attempts to remain righteous through keeping the Law continually fell short, which was why sacrifices had to be offered on their behalf. This was where Jesus entered the picture.

God saw that man was not able to keep the Law, so He made a better way. He sent Jesus to become the ultimate blood sacrifice for mankind once and for all. As a result of what Jesus has done, we now have access to the free gift of righteousness through our faith in Him. This means that we are righteous not because of anything we do, but we are made righteous through the finished work of Christ that we receive by faith. We are now under the covenant of grace, which means that God has equipped us with the supernatural ability to overcome sin and every other attack of the enemy. We are no longer bound by condemnation or a sin-consciousness.

*We are righteous not because of anything we do,
but we are made righteous through the finished work
of Christ that we receive by faith.*

People who try to live by the Law will inevitably fall short of their goal, and will develop a self-righteous and judgmental attitude not only toward those outside the church but also toward other Christians. God doesn't want division in the church. Yet religious attitudes have caused monumental strife and separation within the Body of Christ. The division can range from disputes between denominations to disagreements regarding doctrines and everything in between. For example, I've seen Charismatics look down on people who don't attend a Word of Faith church. They believe that if you don't attend this type of church, you don't know God the same way they do. Even when it comes to having understanding about certain aspects of the Word of God, Christians can become extremely judgmental toward those who may not be as spiritually developed or have obtained certain "revelations" from the Word. Unfortunately, people argue over petty issues that cause division. The Apostle Paul had to deal with the same issues that we face today.

In 1 Corinthians 3:1, he says, "However, Brethren, I could not talk to you as to spiritual [men], but as to nonspiritual [men of the flesh, in whom the carnal nature predominates], as to mere infants [in the new life] in Christ [unable to talk yet!]" (AMP). These believers operated in a fleshly, carnal mind-set that kept them trapped in an immature state where the things of God were concerned.

Paul goes on to say in verses 2–7:

> *I fed you with milk, not solid food, for you were not yet strong enough [to be ready for it]; but even yet you are not strong enough [to be ready for it]. For you are still [unspiritual, having the nature] of the flesh [under the control of ordinary impulses]. For as long as [there are] envying and jealousy and wrangling and factions among you, are you not unspiritual and of the flesh, behaving yourselves after a human standard and like mere (unchanged) men? For when one says, I belong to Paul, and another, I belong to Apollos, are you not [proving yourselves] ordinary (unchanged) men? What then is Apollos? What is Paul? Ministering servants [not heads of parties] through whom you believed, even as the Lord appointed to each his task: I planted, Apollos watered, but God [all the while] was making it grow and [He] gave the increase. So*

neither he who plants is anything nor he who waters, but
[only] God Who makes it grow and become greater. (AMP)

These Christians were controlled by their sinful human nature.
They were acting on the evil impulses of envy, jealousy, and strife,
and saying, "I'm better than you because I go to Apollos's church
and you don't." That's not spiritual, and this attitude does not line
up with the Word. Paul called them ordinary, unchanged men
because, with the strife and jealousy among them, they had not
yet received the life-changing power of God.

When you compare doctrinal differences to demonstrate that
you are more spiritual than someone else, and then judge others
by your standard, you are only demonstrating your immaturity.
Likewise, when your judgmental attitude causes division and strife,
you show your lack of knowledge of the Word, and development
in the love of God. This is a common "side effect" of being more
consumed with religion than you are with your relationship with
God, who is love.

A person who shuns judgmental attitudes and embraces living
a life of love would know that God doesn't prefer one person
above another or hold someone higher than the next. God is not
a respecter of persons (see Romans 2:11), and His grace has been
made available to all people. Proverbs 24:23 says, "It is not good
to have respect of persons in judgment." In 1 Corinthians 3:8,
Paul says, "He who plants and he who waters are equal (one in
aim, of the same importance and esteem)" (AMP). God is the one
who causes increase to come.

God doesn't prefer one person above another or hold
someone higher than the next.

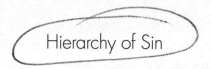

Hierarchy of Sin

Have you ever tried to compare one sin against another sin, making one seem less serious than the other? A person could say to himself, *Okay, so I smoke a little marijuana every now and then. At least I don't do hardcore drugs like Jim does.* By giving different sins different degrees of wickedness, religion allows a person to feel good about the sin that he participates in, which makes it easier to condemn others who are perceived as committing worse sins. Religion judges people and ranks their sins based on an invisible scale.

Religion allows a person to feel good about the sin that he participates in, which makes it easier to condemn others who are perceived as committing worse sins.

Traditional Christians who assign degrees to sin determine who is accepted and who isn't. For example, when a prostitute comes to the church seeking direction, the traditional church will do their best to crucify her. She will be ostracized and quickly pushed back into the world. The church looks at this woman's sin as being at the top of the sin totem pole. After driving her off, they feel good about their own sins because they have told themselves that what they are doing is nowhere near as "bad" as this person's sin. These same people can be causing sedition within the church.

For instance, having sex before marriage often goes under the radar while a young woman who becomes pregnant outside of marriage is shunned, avoided, and run out of the church. Men who physically abuse their wives are excused because they have "anger issues," however, child molesters should be burned at the stake. Sexual sins, such as adultery and homosexuality, are considered to be at the high end of the sin scale by most Christians, while smoking cigarettes, drinking alcohol, cursing, gossiping, and lying are considered minimal.

This phony scale has allowed those who adhere to it to become comfortable in their sin. You see, homosexuality and adultery are quantifiable sins: either you are gay or you're not; either you are cheating on your spouse or you're faithful. The other sins, such as smoking, drinking, and pornography, are considered smaller sins because they are seen as not hurting anyone and can be easily hidden. This has misled people into thinking they are getting away with something because no one knows about it. This is true only from man's standpoint. God weighs the heart as well as the action. He knows the secret thoughts and sees all hidden sins.

God weighs the heart as well as the action. He knows the secret thoughts and sees all hidden sins.

Take adultery, for example. If a married man gets caught in the act of adultery, it's a bad situation for him because it has come out in the open. But if he sits at his desk every day at work and fantasizes in his mind about being intimate with his secretary, he is just as wrong as if he committed the actual act. He thinks because he's not hurting anyone, he hasn't committed a sin. This is a religious idea that contradicts the Word.

Jesus says in Matthew 5:27–28, "You have heard that it was said, You shall not commit adultery. But I say to you that everyone who so much as looks at a woman with evil desire for her has already committed adultery with her in his heart" (AMP). Imagining a sexual encounter with anyone other than your spouse is just as much a sin as the physical act. Even though no one around you knows you are having lustful thoughts, God knows.

If this man is born again and has made Jesus the final authority over His life, this hidden sin will eat him. He'll constantly battle guilt and condemnation. The sad thing is, he can't tell anyone because it's his dirty little secret. Unless he renews his mind and finds out that he has the blood-bought right to receive forgiveness for his sins, he'll be trapped in a cycle of sin and condemnation. Not only are sexual fantasies of equal value to the actual act, but their effects are just as damaging. Though carnal-minded people have determined the severity of each sin, God does not categorize it. To Him, sin is sin.

Religious Clichés Don't Help

To make matters worse, Christians who judge others use powerless religious clichés to try to make others "feel" better about themselves. It is the Word that heals, cleanses, and sets people free, not a church catchphrase.

> *It is the Word that heals, cleanses, and sets people free, not a church catchphrase.*

Telling people who are broken by sin, "Turn it over to Jesus, and He'll work it out," or "Jesus will fix it after a while," doesn't help. Now there may be some element of truth in these sayings, but what people need is wisdom from the Word of God regarding their specific situation. They need the Word broken down so they can understand and apply it to their lives right now. Saying "Joy cometh in the morning" won't help anyone. All people want to know is what is joy, where will it come from, and why they need it. Once you direct people to the Word, show them Scriptures dealing with joy, and give them a chance to meditate and study the Word, then they will understand and know that joy comes from the Word of God that they know and have in operation in their lives.

If you tell people who are caught up in sin that sin doesn't have to dominate their lives anymore because they have God on their side, they can take that knowledge and break sin's power and receive deliverance. A side effect of sin is a feeling of guilt and condemnation. These feelings can cause people to stay in their sin because they don't feel worthy to go before God. If someone would take the time to tell them that there is no condemnation to those who are in Christ Jesus, they would be delivered from those feelings (see Rom. 8:1) and run to God for the strength that they need. Instead, religious Christians want to pacify them by saying, "It's okay, honey, for all have sinned and fallen short of the glory of God. No one is perfect except our Lord Jesus Christ." Counsel such as this doesn't help anyone.

Condemned Christians need to know that although everyone has sinned, everyone can be made righteous. It's the Word of God, not religious clichés, that brings deliverance and changes lives. Instead of giving people the Word, religion judges and gives the world the wrong impression of Christianity and what it is all about. This causes unbelievers to view the church as hypocrites and ultimately turns them away from God.

It's the Word of God, not religious clichés, that brings deliverance and changes lives.

The unsaved see their Christian co-workers talking about the love of God on one day and condemning others the next day. If a carnal-minded Christian learns that her unsaved co-worker is living with her boyfriend, the Christian condemns the person by saying, "Honey, you and your boyfriend are going to burn in hell." Even if they had a close relationship before and the Christian was trying to lead the other woman to Christ, she will now distance herself from the woman and want nothing to do with her. This type of judgmental attitude won't win anyone to Jesus. In fact, it's usually a turnoff to the unsaved.

Understand that sinning is what sinners do. They know that what they are doing is not right and don't need their sin thrown in their faces as a reminder or a weapon used against them. What could possibly stop sinners from sinning? The love of God that is shown to them through Christians will draw sinners to God. The correct response to the situation mentioned before is for the Christian woman to intercede for the young woman in her prayer time and to continue to show the love of God to her. God has given us the ability to judge what is right and what is wrong, but ultimate judgment is His, not ours, to make. Christians should be known for their love, not for condemning people about their sins. Jesus said in John 13:35, "By this shall all men know that ye are my disciples, if ye have love one to another."

> *God has given us the ability to judge what is right and what is wrong, but ultimate judgment is His, not ours, to make.*

First Corinthians 13:4–5 has this to say about love: "[It] does not display itself haughtily. It is not conceited (arrogant and inflated with pride); it is not rude (unmannerly) and does not act unbecomingly" (AMP). Love is not rude or arrogant. Therefore, Christians who imitate God, who is love, should not be rude or arrogant either (see 1 John 4:16). If we are to win this world for Christ, we are going to have to shed our condemning religious ways and develop in the love of God. Leave judgment to Him and let love govern your thoughts and actions.

For by grace are ye saved through faith, and
that not of yourselves: *it is* the gift of God; Not
of works, lest any man should boast. For we are
his workmanship, created in Christ Jesus unto
good works, which God hath before ordained
that we should walk in them.

EPHESIANS 2:8–10

Being then made free from sin, ye became the
servants of righteousness.

ROMANS 6:18

If we confess our sins, he is faithful and just
to forgive us *our* sins and forgive us of all
unrighteousness.

1 JOHN 1:9

REASON #7: RELIGION MAKES PEOPLE TRY TO EARN THEIR WAY TO HEAVEN

Have you ever heard the old saying, "Every charitable act is a stepping-stone toward heaven"? The belief that a person has to do good things to get into heaven has been part of a traditional mind-set for centuries and continues to be prevalent today. Many Christians believe they have to perform good deeds so they can score "points" with God. They volunteer, not because it's good and honorable to help others, but because they think their good deeds will somehow cause God to look more favorably on them. They'll say to themselves, "I helped feed the hungry, and I gave money to the poor. God sees all of this—maybe He'll erase some of my sins."

This type of thinking only keeps people in bondage by making them believe that it's their responsibility to clean themselves up after they've missed the mark. Often, they feel unworthy to participate in church activities because they think God is mad at them. Consequently, their church attendance falls by the wayside, they avoid other believers, and they neglect spending personal time with the Lord. Religion makes people believe that they must be flawless before they approach God. Thinking like this keeps them from going to Him in the first place.

Many believers, as well as unbelievers, are under the impression that they must stop lying, smoking, and sleeping around before they can come to God, but that is far from the truth. I've heard people use the excuse, "I'm just waiting to get myself together before I go to church because I don't want to keep disappointing God." The thing is, you can't clean your life up on your own. If you could, then there would have been no need for Jesus to die on the cross.

I'm Not Worthy

One of the most challenging things I deal with as a pastor is seeing faithful church members fall by the wayside because they feel as though they have messed up and have disappointed God. Because they are more focused on their sin than on their righteousness, they feel too condemned to come back to church. In their minds, they perceive their sin as being beyond God's ability to help, so they sever their relationship with Him.

Several years ago I was at a local mall where I bumped into one of my church members. This was a guy who sat in the second row of every service and never missed a convention at the church. He was a faithful and active member, but after he had become tangled up in sin, he stopped coming to service completely; it was as if he had fallen off the map and disappeared. Instead of receiving God's forgiveness, this young man ran away from Him.

When he saw me, he looked surprised and a little uncomfortable. After some hesitation, he came over to shake my hand. I told him that I hadn't seen him for some time and asked where he had been. He became nervous and started stuttering. He said,

"Well, I, uh, I don't know what happened. I just hit a rough patch, I guess. I got caught up in some mess, which I'm now trying to work through. I know God isn't happy with me, and I should be in church, but I'm trying to get my life together before I come back. I want to get my life right before I go to God."

That's backward! If he had taken the time to renew his mind about what the Word says regarding righteousness, he would have immediately run *to* God, accepting forgiveness, instead of running away from Him. He believed the lie that he wasn't good enough to stand before his heavenly Father. Guilt and condemnation, which are products of sin, were ripping his heart and mind apart. I knew the devil was telling him that he wasn't worthy to ever show his face to God again because he had messed up one too many times.

I said, "Son, let me tell you this: You'll never be good enough. That's why Jesus died on the cross for you. Even though you messed up, you are born again, and you are already right with God. He loves you. He isn't mad at you. If you will look to Jesus, He will help you out."

God is the only one who can turn your life around, not you. He loves you regardless of how many times you mess up. If people would only make a quality decision to get back in His presence, He would completely restore them and turn their situations into a testimony to deliver others.

Contrary to what you may think, sin is not the church's biggest problem. In fact, it should not be a problem for any born-again Christian. Because we have been set free from sin and are now servants of righteousness (see Rom. 6:18). It isn't a sin problem that gets people in trouble; the problem is a religious mind-set that keeps them bound in sin and weakened by guilt and condemnation.

Believers must understand that sin lost its power on the

cross. Jesus redeemed you from the curse of sin once and for all. Romans 8:3 says, "For God…Sending His own Son in the guise of sinful flesh and as an offering for sin, [God] condemned sin in the flesh [subdued, overcame, deprived it of its power over all who accept that sacrifice]" (AMP). Jesus bore your sins at Calvary. His flesh and blood sacrifice secured your righteousness forever.

If you don't already know, righteousness is a free gift from Jesus. You cannot earn it. As a righteous person, you have a right to go before God, and by faith accept the forgiveness that Jesus has already provided. Righteousness is being able to stand before a holy God without a sense of guilt or inferiority, not because of anything *you* did but because of what Jesus did. To wallow in sin, rather than run to God for forgiveness and deliverance, which has already been provided, is a slap in His face.

God has made provision for you to live sin-free as well as guilt-free. His grace is an empowerment that equips you to live a life that pleases Him and allows you to serve Him acceptably. All you have to do is receive His grace by faith and believe that you have everything you need, through Jesus Christ, to live a victorious life. Throw that depression, guilt, and condemnation out the window! You should be rejoicing because you know that when you sin, or miss the mark, you have a right to be forgiven and to keep moving toward God's perfect plan for your life. You may have been sidetracked by sin, but you can repent, change directions, and quickly get back on the right path. The Word says, "Therefore, [there is] now no condemnation (no adjudging guilty of wrong) for those who are in Christ Jesus, who live [and] walk not after the dictates of the flesh, but after the dictates of the Spirit" (Rom. 8:1 AMP). I believe that there is no condemnation for those who are in Christ Jesus, period.

Yes, You Are Worthy—You're Righteous

The Word of God says that believers are now servants of righteousness, but many people can't receive that truth because religion has trained them to think they are just sinners who are saved by grace. They have a hard time being called righteous, because they have taken Romans 3:10 out of context: "There is none righteous, no, not one." The Apostle Paul was talking about unbelievers here, not Christians. Unfortunately, many people still feel as though they must do something to be *righteous*, or to be "in right standing with God." They have not realized that their righteousness was secured on the cross along with their redemption from sin. First Corinthians 1:30 says, "But of him are ye in Christ Jesus, who of God is made unto us wisdom, and righteousness, and sanctification, and redemption."

To overcome this type of mind-set, Christians will have to reject the teaching that says they are righteous through works. Doing goody-goody things like selling fish dinners for the church's building fund or visiting the sick in the hospital do not make you righteous. Take a look at James 2:17–26:

> *In the same way, faith by itself, if it is not accompanied by action, is dead. But someone will say, "You have faith; I have deeds." Show me your faith without deeds, and I will show you my faith by what I do... do you want evidence that faith without deeds is useless? Was not our ancestor Abraham considered righteous for what he did when he offered his son Isaac on the altar? You see that his faith and his actions were working together, and his faith was made complete by what he did. And the scripture was fulfilled that says, "Abraham*

believed God, and it was credited to him as righteousness,"
and he was called God's friend. You see that a person is justi-
fied by what he does and not by faith alone...As the body
without the spirit is dead, so faith without deeds is dead. (NIV)

James said that it is faith that makes a person righteous, and
that person has to have works to show that his faith is operative.
It's not a person's good deeds that get him into heaven; it is a person's faith, supported by his works, that makes him able to stand
confidently before God. Works alone won't get the job done.

Righteousness is something that must be received by faith. You
don't earn it by performing works. It is received when you accept
Jesus as your Lord and Savior. Because of wrong teaching, people
have a hard time understanding what righteousness is and how it
benefits them.

God has set fivefold ministry gifts in the church to help build
up the Body of Christ so that it can come to a place of maturity;
however, many ministers who stand in the offices of pastor, evan-
gelist, teacher, prophet, and apostle don't always do what they
have been called to do. In fact, many men and women of God
have done more harm than good by not rightly dividing the Word.

Take, for instance, the teaching that "All have sinned and come
short of the glory of God," which is based on Romans 3:23. Everyone has heard a message based on this Scripture at one time or
another. Taken out of context, it is one that many preachers use to
justify their willful sin. The truth is that the devil knows what the
Bible says and always takes part of the truth and twists it in order
to justify sin. Satan has used this Scripture to create sin consciousness, which keeps people condemned and in bondage:

But now the righteousness of God without the law is mani-
fested, being witnessed by the law and the prophets; Even the

*righteousness of God which is by faith of Jesus Christ unto all
and upon all them that believe: for there is no difference: For
all have sinned, and come short of the glory of God.* (Romans
3:21–23)

If you look at verse 21, you'll see the Apostle Paul's topic was
the righteousness of God, not sin, as many ministers of the Bible
have taught. What you often hear preached Sunday after Sunday
is an excuse to sin, instead of a push from the pulpit to live a holy
and separated life for God. When a minister is caught red-handed
for sexual immorality, you may hear him say, "Well, you know, all
have sinned and come short of the glory of God." It becomes very
easy for this attitude to trickle down to the members who say,
"Well, you know, praise the Lord, I cussed her out, but you know,
we all have sinned..."

It has come to a point in the Body of Christ where people are
so sin-conscious that they ask God to forgive them of sins even
though they haven't done anything wrong! You hear people pray,
"Lord, forgive me for the sins that I don't know about." What do
they mean by the sin they don't know about? People know when
they sin. But we're more sin-conscious than we are righteousness-
conscious and that's not what God wants for His people.

Job is a perfect example of this. In Job 1:1–22, Job goes before
God and repeatedly makes sacrifices to cover the sins of his children. He does this, not because his children have sinned, but
because he wants to have them covered just in case they sin. Fear
is motivating his actions. Unfortunately, his children die. If Job
was always praying for their forgiveness, why did his children die?
It was because Job's doubt and unbelief gave Satan the right to
wreak havoc in his life.

According to Romans 3:22, Christians receive their righteousness by faith. But many Christians skip over this verse and focus

on verse 23, which says that all have sinned. They overlook the topic of that passage, never realizing that Paul isn't condemning Christians, rather he is saying that everyone has the potential to become righteous through accepting God's free gift. Verse 23 should never be read by itself. Alone, the whole meaning and proper context are missed. Remember, verse 22 says, "For there is no difference." Sin was made available to everyone, and now, through Jesus, righteousness is available to everyone. We all must choose.

All those years of going to church and hearing the wrong message about how we all have sinned and have come short of the glory of God can be thrown out the window. That's not the message that God wants to convey. Everyone who believes in Jesus can choose righteousness over sin. Righteousness is your victory over sin, and it puts you in right standing with God.

The Sea of Forgetfulness

Now that you know you have the *right* to be righteous, let's look at the benefits of righteousness. Contrary to popular belief, righteousness does not give a person a license to sin. Some Christians grab hold of 1 John 1:9: "If we confess our sins, he is faithful and just to forgive us our sins, and to cleanse us from all unrighteousness" and use it as a "Get Out of Jail for Free" card. They'll say, "Lord, forgive me for taking those drugs," then at the first opportunity they get, they get high again. They try to use the righteousness and mercy of God to continue living a sinful lifestyle.

Please understand, Christians shouldn't be looking for a way to sin, but instead, they should be looking for a way out of sin. When you have a revelation of God's grace, which empowers you *not* to sin, you will find yourself walking in perpetual victory over those mind-sets and behaviors that held you back in your walk with God. Your righteousness doesn't allow you to sin, but it does allow you to have confidence in knowing that God has forgiven you when you do miss the mark. Also, when you know you are righteous, you know that you don't have to sin if you don't want to. Jesus has made you free from the law of sin and death, and you are no longer in the prison of sin. You are in the prison of righteousness!

Missing the mark is inevitable at first. Even mature Christians miss it at times, in one area or another. As much as a person wants to walk perfectly before God, that doesn't always happen. Please know, just because you're righteous doesn't mean that issues won't come up in your life that will tempt you to get out of line. Some situations will even cause you to stumble and fall. But the important thing to remember is to avoid getting stuck in a fallen position. The Bible says to arise, or get into a new position. You can't stay on the ground, beaten and defeated. You have to brush yourself off and keep going. As a child of God, you have a blood-bought right to forgiveness of your sins and the ability to stand in His presence free of all guilt.

You have a right to go to your heavenly Father when you miss it and say, "Lord, help me. I repent. Clean me up," and keep on going. God doesn't act the way we do when we are hurt by others. People tend to hold on to offenses. We may say that we forgive a person, but we'll keep remembering what he or she did to us. On the other hand, once you repent, God chooses not to remember your sins anymore. Psalm 103:12 says, "As far as the east is from the west, so far hath he removed our transgressions from us." God has separated you from sin so that you can come boldly to His throne, but you'll back away from it every time *if* you don't allow righteousness to dominate your thinking.

Some people think that because I am a pastor, I must be

perfect. They think that I float on a cloud when I walk and that I never make a mistake. My wife, Taffi, will be the first to tell you that that is far from the truth! I'm far from perfect, and I'll occasionally miss the mark. Yet I am open to receive correction from God or from my wife when I'm wrong. In doing so, I'm growing, learning, and preparing for the next obstacle that comes my way. I'm passing the tests that are before me so I can graduate to the next level. You have to use temptations and conflicts as opportunities to learn and grow instead of allowing them to be stumbling blocks and hindrances to God's perfect plan for you.

There are people who think they're no longer born again because they repeatedly miss the mark. No! As believers, we already knew going into this thing that we are not perfect. That's why we had to go in through Jesus. He is the only one who is perfect. Once we made this connection with Jesus, we received an Advocate with the Father through whom we can have forgiveness of our sins. As a result, when we miss the mark, we can receive forgiveness made available by the blood of Jesus, which has already been applied to cleanse us from all of our sins. For this reason, we can continue to move on in the righteousness of God.

There are some people who think, "Well, you know what? God's not going to use me or speak to me because I sinned." That's simply not true. I can go through Scripture after Scripture and show them all the people whom God spoke to right after they missed it. Look at King David. He was an adulterer and a murderer, yet God called him a man after His own heart.

If you condemn yourself and continue to say, "I'm not worthy or perfect enough to hear from the Lord," you disqualify yourself from being used. Do you have to be flawless in order for

God to use you? No! If you'll take advantage of the blood that was shed by Jesus and stand with confidence in your righteousness, He will.

> *Do you have to be flawless in order for God to use you? No!*

So you sinned. Now what? Most people start to wallow in a "pity party" and feel guilty for what they did. Don't even go there. Right in the midst of your situation, before your pity party starts, begin to thank the Lord for His forgiveness. Say, "Thank You, Jesus, for being here for me. Through You, I'm saved, and I have the grace of God to be forgiven." I'm telling you that by the time you finish bringing the issue to God, He will be speaking to you!

Instead of people getting back in God's presence to hear His answers, the Body of Christ wants to get to God through their good works. Understand, you can never be good enough, work hard enough, or do enough charity work to get into heaven. You must go through Jesus; He's the only way to the Father. This revelation didn't come to me right away. Like others who grew up in the church, I thought good deeds were the key to getting into heaven. Then one day I realized that wasn't right, and that it wasn't biblical. I thought to myself: *As hard as I work to be flawless and perfect, my righteousness isn't dependent upon my actions, because even if I were perfect, without Jesus, I still wouldn't be good enough.* I'm not righteous without Him. I can't hear without Him. My faith can't work without Him. That's why it's nonsense for people to think they can earn their way to heaven through good works. Everything is based on your acceptance of Jesus.

Good Without God Doesn't Add Up

Have you ever heard the argument from a person who says, "I'm a good person at heart. I don't drink alcohol, smoke, or take illegal drugs. I'm kind to others. So why do I need to know Jesus?" People who say that are generally law-abiding citizens with what the world considers good morals. They think that their many gifts of time and money given to charitable organizations and good causes make them good enough to go to heaven, despite the fact that they haven't accepted Jesus as their Lord and Savior. They are in for a rude awakening when they reach hell and realize that they had been living a lie.

This type of thinking isn't limited to the world either. There are those who have gone to church all of their lives, yet have not accepted Christ. They feel their place in heaven is secured because they are faithful in the choir or have served in the church for twenty years. These kinds of people work their fingers to the bone in ministry positions and do good works in the community, but don't realize that it's all in vain if they don't invite Jesus into their hearts.

People must realize that being good without having God doesn't equal going to heaven. God must be behind everything that you do; He must be your motivator.

God must be behind everything that you do;
He must be your motivator.

According to a 2000 Barna Research Group survey, 57 percent of all adults and three out of five teens (61 percent) who don't attend church believe that if a person is generally good, or does enough good things for others during his or her life, that person will earn a place in heaven. In addition, a study by the same group in 2004 found that more than half of all adults (saved and unsaved) also agree with that statement. This is a sad statistic. So many people have been deceived by wrong religious teachings. The church must rid itself of all traces of religion and get busy spreading the truth of salvation and the gospel of grace if these people are ever going to be free from bondage.

When the church begins to understand that no amount of service can outweigh Jesus' sacrifice for you or me, people will begin to live their lives differently. Good works would be performed to glorify God instead of trying to get attention from Him. People's hearts would change as well as their motivation for the things that they do. The best benefit of understanding your righteousness is knowing that even though you may mess up and sin, God still loves you, and you have a right to cry out to Him, "Abba, Father." He will be there to help you every step of the way.

> *When the church begins to understand that no amount of service can outweigh Jesus' sacrifice for you or me, people will begin to live their lives differently.*

Remember, it's not your good works that open the gates of heaven. Jesus is the key, and unless you go through Him, you'll never see that promise: "Jesus saith unto him, I am the way, the truth, and the life: no man cometh unto the Father, but by me" (John 14:6). Accept Him today and receive the best gift you could ever have—right standing with God.

The Lord *is* gracious, and full of compassion; slow
to anger, and of great mercy.
The Lord *is* good to all; and his tender mercies *are*
over all his works.

PSALM 145:8-9

These things I have spoken unto you, that in me
ye might have peace. In the world ye shall have
tribulation: but be of good cheer; I have overcome
the world.

JOHN 16:33

For I am persuaded, that neither death, nor life,
nor angels, nor principalities, or powers, nor
things present, nor things to come,
Nor height, nor depth, nor any other creature,
shall be able to separate us from the love of God,
which is Christ Jesus our Lord.

ROMANS 8:38-39

REASON #6: RELIGION PROMOTES THE IDEA THAT GOD USES CALAMITY TO TEACH HIS PEOPLE

Why is it that when a person is faced with a tough situation or things aren't going his way in life, he is quick to blame God? People often ask, "Why is the Lord doing this to me?" From their car breaking down to being laid off from work to being diagnosed with a major illness, people have always placed the fault on God when things don't go right. Before I ever received revelation and understanding of the Word, I would think the same thing: *Why does God punish people?* Because of a lack of understanding, people quickly fall into a traditional mind-set and say, "Well, God must be trying to teach me something," or "Maybe He's punishing me for something bad that I've done." But that way of thinking is wrong. The truth is: God doesn't operate that way. Because of people's religious view of who God is, they automatically assume that He's behind everything—good or bad.

Religion has taught people that God is an irate dictator who rules the world with an iron fist. It teaches that He is just waiting for you to make one wrong move so He can punish you by sending you through a series of difficult tests and trials. Religion also implies that God is not above using sickness, financial woes, and even the death of a loved one to develop a person's patience or faith. Because believers feel that God is the one causing all the trouble in their lives, they happily put up with these situations, as if they're doing their Christian duty to suffer, instead of taking authority over the situations.

This false view of God has created a doctrine of suffering that has been seared into the minds of believers and unbelievers alike. People willingly suffer through troubled times and wear their battle scars as a badge of honor. They believe that it is God's will for Christians to suffer, and they have also been conditioned to accept struggle and hardship as part of the package deal for serving God.

Hearing numerous songs and sermons glorifying the plight of the Christian has built mental strongholds in the minds of many people. These strongholds perpetuate the idea that every trial a person faces and suffers through is all part of God's perfect plan for his or her life. Sickness, lack, spiritual bondage, and even death are all generally accepted as God's will. There is no acknowledgment of the devil, or even people's own bad decisions. The truth is that God never intended for His people to suffer; that's just not who He is. He loves us, and He wants the very best for us, which includes an abundant life of success and fulfillment.

The truth is that God never intended for His people to suffer; that's just not who He is.

God is a loving God, unlike many of the predominant deities of other religions. In Greek mythology, Zeus, the chief god, was said to hurl lightning bolts down in judgment at those who angered him. Islam says that sometimes bad things happen to believers for their own good, giving them a chance to think about what they've done wrong. But when you serve the one true God, you can take comfort in knowing that He doesn't hand out disease to those who commit adultery or dish out financial disaster to those who lie. Our God is forgiving and just when we repent. He even shows mercy to us when we don't deserve it. Everything good that He does is designed to bring us into a closer relationship with Him.

Please understand, there are consequences that come with sin; however, those consequences are more about the natural progression of continuing down the wrong path than they are about God doling out the punishment. When we open the door to the enemy through disobedience, he can gain a foothold in our lives, which is why God doesn't want us participating in sin. The key to remember is that God does not use evil to bring about good because that would go against His very nature.

> *God does not use evil to bring about good because that would go against His very nature.*

Look at what Jesus had to say to the Pharisees. They had accused Him of casting out devils, healing the sick, and restoring sight to the blind with the assistance of Satan. Jesus said, "Every kingdom divided against itself will be ruined, and every city or household divided against itself will not stand. If Satan drives out Satan, he is divided against himself. How then can his kingdom stand?" (Matt. 12:25–27 NIV). Jesus took the evil— sickness and bondage—off these people and gave them complete restoration. Evil cannot be used to produce good; it's just not possible.

The fact of the matter is that the true culprit behind evil is Satan. In John 10:10, Jesus says, "The thief cometh not, but for to steal, and to kill, and to destroy: I am come that they might have life, and that they might have it more abundantly." Satan is the thief. He is the one who steals, kills, and destroys. Jesus' goal is for you to have an abundant life—one that overflows with goodness.

The proof that God doesn't want you to suffer can be found throughout His Word. Psalm 35:27 says that He takes pleasure in the total life prosperity of His people; therefore, He will not use evil to teach you lessons. God's ultimate goal is for you to be healed, set free, happy, rich, and living an abundant life instead of being sick, broke, busted, and disgusted. God is happy when you are fully supplied, and He wants to show you His goodness. However, He's not just good to believers. The Bible says that He's good to all: "The Lord *is* gracious, and full of compassion; slow to anger, and of great mercy. The Lord *is* good to all: and his tender mercies *are* over all his works" (Ps. 145:8–9).

God's ultimate goal is for you to be healed, set free, happy, rich, and living an abundant life.

The Hard Knock Life of a Christian

Many Christians are resigned to a lifetime of struggles because they feel that it's God's will for them to suffer. They will tolerate hardship after hardship because they think that it is honorable to do so. People even believe that they must suffer for the gospel's sake. This belief is even reflected in the songs that we sing in church.

One of the most popular gospel songs in the traditional church is "Rough Side of the Mountain." The main chorus describes believers making a difficult, treacherous climb up a mountain, trusting God and trying really hard to make it. This song had Christians all across the globe climbing the rough side of the mountain. Yet God never told Christians to climb mountains. In fact, He told them to speak to the mountain, and it would be removed (see Mark 11:23). These religious songs not only contradict the Word of God, but also promote the idea that life is supposed to be a constant struggle when it's not.

When I used to sing in the men's chorus, we sang a song in which the lead singer would start out saying how hard it is to get by and get along in life. Man, we'd get to rocking and shouting. The church would be in a frenzy over that song. Folks would be shouting and saying, "Yes, Lord, it's just so hard!" In that song, we were glorifying hardship and suffering. No wonder the church is confused!

Many believers feel that you can't really know the Lord if you never go through the tests and trials of life, but that's not God's design for any Christian. An old saying in the church is, "Child, if there's no rain in your life, you'll never learn to appreciate the sunshine." To strengthen their case, they'd sing about how we all have a cross to bear. By the time they finished singing, you wondered if you even wanted to be a Christian serving a God who wanted you to suffer.

What people don't understand is that before the foundations of the earth were established, God predestined those who follow Him to experience the good life. Ephesians 2:10 says:

> *For we are God's [own] handiwork (His workmanship), recreated in Christ Jesus, [born anew] that we may do those good works which God predestined (planned beforehand) for us [taking paths which He prepared ahead of time], that*

we should walk in them [living the good life which He pre-
arranged and made ready for us to live]. (AMP)

It's disheartening to see so many preachers talk so much about the pressures of life and about how the only rest a person will have is in heaven. This "No cross, no crown" doctrine is misleading scores of people. The ministers tell their congregations that they have to suffer before they can receive promotion and that God uses trouble and disasters to build character in them. This is wrong teaching; it's just not biblical.

Some people might ask, "Are you trying to tell us that we never have to go through any hard times, Dr. Dollar?" No, I'm not saying that. Jesus did say that there would be tribulation in this world, but He also said to be of good cheer because He overcame the world, depriving it of its power over you (see John 16:33).

> *Jesus did say that there would be tribulation in*
> *this world, but He also said to be of good cheer*
> *because He overcame the world, depriving it of*
> *its power over you.*

I can hear people laughing at me now. They are saying, "Christians don't suffer? Then what do you call my being laid off from work and my wife leaving me? I call that suffering." What I mean is that Christians don't suffer in the same worldly sense that the others do. What we are put through is more of an endurance race. Paul writes in 1 Corinthians 9:24:

Do you not know that in a race all the runners compete, but [only] one receives the prize? So run [your race] that you may lay hold [of the prize] and make it yours. Now every athlete who goes into training conducts himself temperately and restricts himself in all things. They do it to win a wreath that will soon wither, but we [do it to receive a crown of eternal blessedness] that cannot wither. Therefore I do not run uncertainly (without definite aim).

When I played football, my coach taught us that the hardest thing during the whole football season should be the practice; the game should be sweatless. We would practice two to three times a day to prepare for the actual game. Coach knew that if we could just prepare ourselves through practice, the game wouldn't be hard because we had conditioned our bodies and our minds to overcome the pain, frustration, and exhaustion. When we went out on the field for a game, we did what we were trained to do and obtained the victory. But the guy who's out of shape because he refused to practice and train will be unprepared and get the wind knocked out of him on the first play of the game.

There are a lot of "out of shape" Christians who refuse to get up and "practice." They are out of shape in regards to the Word. They are out of confession-shape and out of prayer-shape, and they want to lay the blame on God when the devil knocks the wind out of them. Because they didn't practice the Word, when hardship came, it was able to ruin their lives. Once it was all over, they glorified the hardship and praised God for the lesson they learned and for getting them where they needed to be. They shout, rejoice, and testify to others about their suffering. What they don't realize is that if they would have done what was in the Word in the first place, they could have avoided the whole ordeal.

You've got to begin to renew your mind to what God has already said in His Word. When you are ignorant of what the Word actually says, hardships will come and you won't have any power to overcome them. The Word of God is your power source, but if you haven't filled your heart up with it, you won't be able to stand against the wiles of the devil.

> *You've got to begin to renew your mind to what God has already said in His Word.*

On the other hand, when you prepare yourself by renewing your mind, working the Word, disciplining yourself, and practicing what the Word says, you'll be more than ready to take on the enemy. Ephesians 6:10–17 says:

> *Finally, my brethren, be strong in the Lord, and in the power of his might. Put on the whole armour of God, that ye may be able to stand against the wiles of the devil. For we wrestle not against flesh and blood, but against principalities, against powers, against the rulers of the darkness of this world, against spiritual wickedness in high places. Wherefore take unto you the whole armour of God, that ye may be able to withstand in the evil day, and having done all, to stand. Stand therefore, having your loins girt about with truth, and having on the breastplate of righteousness; And your feet shod with the preparation of the gospel of peace; Above all, taking the shield of faith, wherewith ye shall be able to quench all the fiery darts of the wicked. And take the helmet of salvation, and the sword of the Spirit, which is the word of God.*

Suit up in God's armor so you can easily defeat the devil and whatever he tries to throw your way.

Many Christians are basically glorifying the trials and tribulations they go through instead of standing strong in the authority that God has given them. This practice is widespread, and the sad thing is that people don't understand that there is no glory in the struggles a person goes through. This is a religious concept that has no basis in the Word of God. The glory comes from when you overcome and triumph over the situation. If cancer rears its ugly head, the glory will come after you have spent time in the Word, you've made confessions, and the doctor comes to you saying that you are completely healed. God was the one who brought you out on top. Your hard times don't perfect you. It is God, through His Word, who does the perfecting.

 Your hard times don't perfect you. It is God, through His Word, who does the perfecting.

I remember a time when I came out of a difficult situation all bruised and beaten up, the Spirit of God didn't congratulate me and tell me that this experience made me stronger. He said, "Had you done what I told you to do before all this craziness happened, you wouldn't have had to struggle like that."

I know what you're thinking: *If Christians aren't supposed to suffer through things, then why do bad things happen to good people?* Sometimes, people open the door for bad situations to occur in their lives because of their negative words and attitudes. The Bible says, "Death and life are in the power of the tongue: and they that love it shall eat the fruit thereof" (Prov. 18:21). A person's negative actions will open up the door and allow Satan room to operate in his or her life. A man might think that just because he has been in the church for over thirty years, nothing bad should happen to him. If this person only knows traditional teachings, then his actions aren't Bible-based but fear-based, and fear is the key that the devil needs to operate in your life.

God didn't create sickness, bondage, and lack to punish us. These things are in the world today because of Adam's disobedience in the Garden of Eden. God created man as a free moral agent, giving us the ability to choose between right and wrong. Adam willfully chose to listen to the devil and disobey God's order not to eat the forbidden fruit. Because of his act of disobedience and treason against God, sin, sickness, and suffering entered the world. But through the blood of Jesus, believers now have the right to wholeness, soundness, and peace in their lives. It is because of wrong teaching that many Christians still think God puts affliction on them, so they put up no resistance to it, and are defeated time and time again.

Through the blood of Jesus, believers now have the right to wholeness, soundness, and peace in their lives.

Rom. 8:28

All Things Work Together for Your Good

When Christians are in the midst of their hard times, what religious cliché do you hear repeated the most? People will say, "Well, you know, all things work together for the good of those who love the Lord." My question is: Do all things really work together for your good? Does cancer work for your good? This disease is working twenty-four hours a day and seven days a week to kill you, so how is good supposed to come out of it?

People will pluck Romans 8:28 out of the Bible and use it to justify all their problems: "And we know that all things work together for good to them that love God." What sense does that make? Does your precious little baby dying in a car accident work for your good? We know that the child is in heaven, but he was never able to grow up and fulfill the will of God for his life. Losing your child is never for your good. What about other calamities, such as your house burning down, losing a job, being physically attacked, or being diagnosed with an incurable disease? Do these things work together for your good? You can try to take comfort in that Scripture and say, "Brother, I know that it's working for my good...somehow," but it just won't work.

Do all things work for your good? No. Can God allow something good to come out of a bad situation? Yes! When a person dies unexpectedly, how can God use it for good? This situation will open a door for others to accept Christ into their lives. For example, during home-going services, I always give people an opportunity to give their lives to Christ or to rededicate their lives if they are in a backslidden position. I have seen many lives saved and transformed during these services. That is something to truly rejoice about.

> *Do all things work for your good? No. Can God allow something good to come out of a bad situation? Yes!*

When someone tries to use Romans 8:28 in the wrong context, take the opportunity to share the truth with them. Break the Scripture down in order for them to understand its true meaning. Tell them to look at the whole passage—Romans 8:26–28—instead of just that one verse. When you look at the whole passage, you will see that it is referring to the things of prayer. It says the Spirit of God will help us to pray as we ought to and that all the things of prayer work together for our good. The Holy Spirit, the will of God, and speaking in tongues all work for your good—not all the evil things that happen to you.

God's Best

Don't believe the hype of the suffering doctrine; God only wants His best for you. When you work the Word of God, by studying, confessing, and obeying it, you can go through any trial the devil tries to send your way and be victorious in the end. And although you may have to endure trials, you don't have to set up a tent and camp there. God gave you everything you need to overcome any situation you encounter. Just know that He's not behind the trouble; He's the one who gives you the power to come out.

> *God gave you everything you need to overcome any situation you encounter. Just know that He's not behind the trouble; He's the one who gives you the power to come out.*

Isaiah 54:14–17 says:

You shall establish yourself in righteousness (rightness, in conformity with God's will and order): you shall be far from even the thought of oppression or destruction, for you shall not fear, and from terror, for it shall not come near you. Behold, they may gather together and stir up strife, but it is not from Me. Whoever stirs up strife against you shall fall and surrender to you. Behold, I have created the smith who blows on the fire of coals and who produces a weapon for its purpose; and I have created the devastator to destroy. But no weapon that is formed against you shall prosper, and every tongue that shall rise against you in judgment you shall show to be in the wrong. This [peace, righteousness, security, triumph over opposition] is the heritage of the servants of the Lord [those in whom the ideal Servant of the Lord is reproduced]; this is the righteousness or the vindication which they obtain from Me [this is that which I impart to them as their justification], says the Lord. (AMP)

Peace, righteousness, security, and victory over opposition are your heritage as a believer. Don't ever doubt that God will bring you out of every bad situation. He guarantees that the devil's weapons will not work against you, and He also gives you the ability to be vindicated through Him. His desire for you is to be as successful as you can be in doing this.

Know ye not that ye are the temple of God, and *that* the Spirit of God dwelleth in you?

1 CORINTHIANS 3:16

So then faith *cometh* by hearing, and hearing by the word of God.

ROMANS 10:17

For God is not *the author* of confusion, but of peace, as in all churches of the saints.

1 CORINTHIANS 14:33

Wisdom *is* the principle thing; *therefore* get wisdom: and with all thy getting get understanding.

PROVERBS 4:7

Solomon   James 1:5-8

REASON #5: RELIGION TURNS CHURCH SERVICES INTO FORUMS FOR EMOTIONALISM AND ENTERTAINMENT

After returning from a ministry engagement in South Africa, I began to clearly see some things about the church here in the United States, namely that it seems to be turning into a "circus" with each passing Sunday. Believers are parading around in the church trying to look pious and ultraspiritual without demonstrating the true power of God. Church has become a place where Christians go to get a spiritual "fix" to hold them over until the next Sunday service. They come to church to shout, dance, and fulfill what they perceive as their religious duty. Essentially, church has become a place where people come to be entertained.

It is not uncommon to see people engaging in various displays of outward religious "performances," but when it comes to their ability to execute the Word of God in their personal lives, they fall short. There are preachers who are preaching things that aren't even scriptural, and many churches focus on the spectacular, rather than the supernatural power of God, just to keep the people coming back. There are so many gimmicks in the church that it's ridiculous.

The worst part is that we've taken the Word and tried to turn it into a show. It seems that nobody is interested in hearing the pure, unadulterated Word of God, raw and uncut. I've found that people don't want to hear what God has to say as much as they want to be entertained. But contrary to religious ideas, church is not a form of entertainment; it's not *Showtime at the Apollo*. Church is supposed to be like school. It's a place where you come to learn about the things of God so you can win life's battles when you leave the sanctuary.

Unfortunately, religion has turned church into a "see and be seen" type of gathering where people display their looks and talents, without ever tapping into the true power of God. Christians will pack convention halls to get healed and delivered, but many of the people who desperately need God to show up in their lives are not receiving anything from Him because they are failing to get understanding. We try to make it look as if people are getting delivered in services, but all they are really getting is a dose of high emotionalism. Christians have become quite satisfied with this type of nonsense, and consequently, they stay stuck in their problems and yield to a spirit of despair, only to go back and get another fix the next Sunday. They don't understand that the Word is the needful thing, that it's a manual for living. And because they refuse to seek after the Word, and trust God and His grace, they get addicted to an emotional high.

Overcoming Emotionalism

Have you ever been to a church service that was geared toward getting the congregation hyped up? From the long devotional prayer recitations to the choir's electrifying performances, everything makes you want to jump, shout, dance, and run around the sanctuary, but at the end of the day, you didn't get fed the Word of God.

I'm sure you've been in a service like this before. After the choir delivers a rousing rendition of the Sunday selection, the preacher comes out to deliver his sermon. He opens his Bible and turns to his Scripture text, then closes the Bible and begins his performance. He hoops, hollers, screams like James Brown, throws himself on the pulpit, and marches across the platform while yelling something you can't understand. The problem is he didn't back up any part of his message with Scripture. He merely told the people that they were all on their way to hell, and if they want fire insurance, they'd better get saved and join the church.

The church signals their approval of the message by responding with a chorus of "Amens," "Hallelujahs," and "Praise the Lords." The next thing you know, someone "gets happy" and catches the Spirit. Everything comes to a frantic climax as the choir sings "Come to Jesus," and the preacher opens the doors of the church so people can decide if they want to get saved or not. The problem is that people can't make a sound decision if they are being swept away by their emotions.

Emotions have a God-given role in the life of every believer, but they become dangerous when people try to manipulate them to control or mislead others. Yes, people should be motivated to become born again, but their motivation should be founded on the faith that comes to them when they hear the Word being preached (see Rom. 10:17), not fear or some other intense feeling. Some ministers feel as if they have to use emotions to motivate the people in a church service, but that is not true. Look at the Apostle Paul's ministry:

> *As for myself, brethren, when I came to you, I did not come proclaiming to you the testimony and evidence or mystery*

and secret of God [concerning what He has done through Christ for the salvation of men] in lofty words of eloquence or human philosophy and wisdom; for I resolved to know nothing (to be acquainted with nothing, to make a display of the knowledge of nothing, and to be conscious of nothing) among you except Jesus Christ (the Messiah) and Him crucified. And my language and my message were not set forth in persuasive (enticing and plausible) words of wisdom, but they were in demonstration of the [Holy] Spirit and power [a proof by the Spirit and power of God, operating on me and stirring in the minds of my hearers the most holy emotions and thus persuading them], so that your faith might not rest in the wisdom of men (human philosophy), but in the power of God. (1 Corinthians 2:1–2, 4–5 AMP)

Emotions have a God-given role in the life of every believer, but they become dangerous when people try to manipulate them to control or mislead others.

Paul knew the importance of the people understanding the Word, and once they understood clearly, God could move. He knew that he couldn't save men, but God is the one who draws men's hearts to Him. Proverbs 4:7 says, "Wisdom is the principal thing; therefore get wisdom: and with all thy getting get understanding." He didn't use fancy homiletics or elaborate stories to move the people, but instead, he depended on the power of God to anoint his plain speech.

You may ask what is so wrong about a highly emotional service like the one I described earlier. You may even believe that it is nothing more than the result of the Holy Spirit moving on the people of God. While it is true that the Holy Spirit's presence does

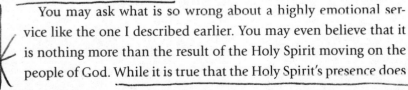

affect your emotions, He does not cause people to get emotionally and physically out of control. Everything that God does is done decently and in order, so if you see someone running through the church "tearing things up" in an unmanageable way, saying the Spirit is moving in him or her, you know that's a lie. That is simply a person who is letting his or her emotions cause this type of reaction. The Holy Spirit is a gentleman, and He won't make you hurt yourself or others.

> *While it is true that the Holy Spirit's presence does affect your emotions, He does not cause people to get emotionally and physically out of control.*

When people get hold of the Word and start studying it, they will see that they have authority over their emotions. They will begin to see that you don't just take everything the preacher says as truth, and that if it's not lining up with God, it should not be received. They won't fall into religious traditions that come from family and friends, but they will begin to experience the true power of God because they have a sure, unshakable foundation on the Word. It will take a hunger and thirst for God to access this power. Unfortunately, many believers are simply not willing to stop playing the religious church games in order to see the anointing become a reality in their lives.

Church Games

I've found over time that many Christians don't actually want the Word, nor do they come to church strictly to be spiritually fed. People may come to church to be seen or even to find a mate.

Many times people get into what I call "church games" and lose sight of the purpose for gathering with fellow believers.

I remember during one of our finance conventions when the Holy Spirit began moving on the hearts of the people, and they started bringing money to the altar. I hadn't seen anything like it before. God prompted the people to sow into the ministry, and they brought their gifts to the altar just like the children of Israel did when they brought freewill offerings to build the tabernacle in Moses' day (see Exod. 36:3). After that service, the giving began to carry over into our regular weekly services.

One Sunday, a member walked up the steps to the pulpit and placed his offering on the podium while I was down in the audience preaching. After that, I noticed people starting to get "deep" with things. Several people now felt as if they had to walk up and put their offering on the podium in order to sow a seed. I would be up there preaching and people would interrupt my teaching to put their envelope on the podium. Then some of them would even gesture to the crowd on their way down the stairs.

The Holy Spirit is not going to tell anyone to interrupt the Word of God as it's going forth, so those people were simply doing something to get attention and "show out" for the camera. These people took something that started out as a move of God and turned it into a show.

My response was to make an announcement that people could no longer bring their offerings up and place them on the pulpit. Let me tell you, when I made that announcement, the number of people who brought offerings down front quickly began to dwindle. They loved being able to walk down to the altar in front of everyone to place their money on the podium, but when they had to put their gifts in the receptacles at the sides of the podium area, where there were no cameras, things changed.

These are the same type of people who get upset when it seems they never get a return on their giving. It is no wonder they never receive a harvest, however, because their hearts weren't in their giving. First Corinthians 13:3 says, "And though I bestow all my goods to feed the poor, and though I give my body to be burned, and have not charity, it profiteth me nothing." You can't sow seeds and expect to receive a harvest if you don't give unselfishly without ulterior motives. Loveless sowing of time, goods, and money won't produce a profit for you even if you give your last dime.

God is always concerned with the heart of the believer rather than the outward display a person portrays. He knows the motives and the intents of your heart. The Bible says:

> [Remember] this: he who sows sparingly and grudgingly will also reap sparingly and grudgingly, and he who sows generously [that blessings may come to someone] will also reap generously and with blessings. Let each one [give] as he has made up his own mind and purposed in his heart, not reluctantly or sorrowfully or under compulsion, for God loves (He takes pleasure in, prizes above other things, and is unwilling to abandon or to do without) a cheerful (joyous, "prompt to do it") giver [whose heart is in his giving]. And God is able to make all grace (every favor and earthly blessing) come to you in abundance, so that you may always and under all circumstances and whatever the need be self-sufficient [possessing enough to require no aid or support and furnished in abundance for every good work and charitable donation]. (2 Corinthians 9:6–8 AMP)

When you give motivated by love, God will cause His blessings to abound, but if you are giving for any other reason, you might as well keep your money.

At the same time, many other people in church continued to sow and received an abundant harvest because love was the motivation behind their giving. They were giving with a joyful heart out of love and obedience to the Father, and they were blessed. Those who received nothing from God got their reward when everyone saw them walking up to sow. God doesn't play games, so there's no room for games in the church.

God doesn't play games, so there's no room
for games in the church.

Perfecting Phoniness

The danger of religion lies in the fact that it perfects phoniness. It takes things that are spiritual and twists them into a form of pretense. It walks a fine line between what is true spirituality and what is flesh-based thinking. That explains why two believers can go to the same church, hear the same sermon, serve in the same volunteer ministry, and get two totally different results from the Word.

One person goes to church hungry for the Word of God, and the other goes to see how many fine men are there that Sunday, which is a carnal motivation for going. Both say "Amen" and "Hallelujah" at the same parts of the message, read the same Bible, give the same amount of money in offering, and serve in the same ministry, yet one experiences the power of God in her life and the other is all form and no power.

It's a sad indictment that the church of Jesus Christ has gotten over into these types of church games. People have perfected phoniness, acting as if they love God and their neighbors, but it's really the complete opposite. They can smile at people in church and gossip about them behind their backs. These kinds of Christians don't know real love, not the God kind of love that should be flowing out from the church and overflowing into the world.

Religion keeps the Body of Christ in a state of immaturity, where hypocrisy and selfishness reign over God's Word. It's caused the love of the people in the church to grow cold, and people don't sincerely love God or those around them. The Bible says that the distinguishing mark of a true Christian is his love for his brothers and sisters, but because believers refuse to grow up in the Word, they stay in a surface, shallow type of love that's based on their flesh.

Romans 12:9 in the New King James Version says, "Let love be without hypocrisy. Abhor what is evil. Cling to what is good." The Amplified Version says, "[Let your] love be sincere (a real thing); hate what is evil [loathe all ungodliness, turn in horror from wickedness], but hold fast to that which is good," while the New Living Translation says, "Don't just pretend that you love others. Really love them. Hate what is wrong. Hold tightly to what is good." But if you won't get in the Word, how can you love those around you or be anything other than a hypocrite?

Every promise or teaching in the Word of God is undergirded by the love of God, so if there is no comprehension of or seeking after the Word, then love will continue to wax cold in the church. If the church is cold and unloving, then where can sinners turn? They're being turned off by the church circus, and they can't find a loving believer, so they stay disconnected from Jesus—the only one who can really help them. All of this is a result of having turned church into an entertainment showcase.

If the church is cold and unloving, then where can sinners turn?

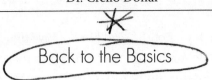

Back to the Basics

Change is not that far off if the Body of Christ would just get back to the basics of their faith in Jesus Christ. If believers would start opening their Bibles and reading them for themselves, they would have the power of God flowing in their lives on a consistent basis instead of this hit-or-miss traditional mess that is going on now. And if preachers would stop preaching what they think the people want to hear and, instead, start preaching what the Spirit of the Lord is really saying, our churches would be packed with people who are hungry for the power of God and demonstrating that power in their lives.

When I started World Changers Church, in New York City, I let the church know up front that I don't play church games. I give them the Word and nothing else. I'm not going to rhyme or jump through hoops to keep them coming to church. If people can't hear and understand what I am saying when I preach, how can faith come?

It doesn't matter if I talk in a calm manner or shout as loud as I can, it won't make the words any more anointed. When you preach according to how God called you, you will get results. I don't preach a sermon to get a "10" or to get people's approval. I want God to approve of me. I am, however, going to trust God to build leaders in this fellowship who know how to use the Word as a recipe book to whip the devil and everything he throws at them.

When you preach according to how God called you, you will get results.

When sickness comes, they will know to immediately go to 1 Peter 2:24, which says, "By whose [Jesus'] stripes ye were healed." They will know that if they honor the Lord with all their increase, that they will be blessed to be a blessing (see Prov. 3:9–10, Gen. 12:1–3). They will be well equipped in the Word and more than conquerors in this world. They will trust Jesus and lean on His undeserved favor for everything.

My prayer is that every Christian will turn back to their first love, turn back to the Word, and turn away from hyper-emotionalism. I also pray that every minister will begin to take seriously the call of God on his life and stop prostituting the gospel of Jesus Christ for personal gain or to build up their self-image. It's not about you. It's about Jesus and souls being saved.

Never forget that *minister* means "servant." Church is a place to serve the people of God and to perfect them for the work of the ministry. It is not the place to gain adoration or accolades from them. It is wrong for a minister to use his gifts to glorify himself rather than to glorify God.

We need to start preaching the Word in season and out, when it's popular and when it's not, because Jesus is on His way back. We are living in the last sliver of time before our Lord and Savior returns, and we must be ready for the harvest of souls that is on its way into the kingdom of God. Get away from this traditional method of having church and get before God for His wisdom and revelation. A highly charged emotional environment is not necessarily an indication that the anointing is present.

If you want to transform your life and the life of your unsaved friends and loved ones, get in the presence of God by getting in His Word, not the realm of emotions. While emotions do have their place, a religious, emotional show in church won't get the job done, but will only leave you feeling the same way you felt when you came in the church doors. The Word, on the other hand, will feed your spirit and give you the tools you need to succeed in life.

If you want to transform your life and the life of your unsaved friends and loved ones, get in the presence of God by getting in His Word.

Therefore I say unto you, Whatever things soever
ye desire, when ye pray, believe that ye receive
them, and ye shall have *them*.

MARK 11:24

But when ye pray, use not vain repetitions, as
the heathen do: for they think that they shall be
heard for their much speaking. Be not ye therefore
like unto them: for your Father knoweth what
things ye have need of, before ye ask him.

MATTHEW 6:7–8

But without faith it is impossible to please *him*;
for he that cometh to God must believe that he is,
and *that* he is a rewarder of them that diligently
seek him.

HEBREWS 11:6

REASON #4: RELIGION TURNS PRAYER INTO A "FORM OF GODLINESS" WITH NO POWER

Have you ever had a need and prayed to God, but your prayer went unanswered and your need remained unmet? You may have pleaded with God, saying, "Lord I need you; my baby needs a pair of shoes and I got a light bill due. My telephone is disconnected, and I can't wait until my next paycheck. I need some money right now, Lord. I need you now, Jesus. Help me, Jesus! Help me!" Sound familiar? Everyone has been here at one point or another. Prayers like these are emotional, and they don't move God. He is, however, moved by faith. It is the only way to get results in God's kingdom. Religion, on the other hand, turns prayer into an outward display of emotion that has no power behind it.

I know Christians who pray and cry, thinking: *Surely God will move on my behalf, because He knows how much I need Him.* But after all that was said and done, the money never came in, and eventually they got angry with God. They thought God was able to help them, but they didn't see any results. They thought, *Doesn't God know what I need before I ask Him?*

On that point, they're right. The Bible does say in Matthew 6:8

that God knows what you need before you ask, but you have to ask according to His Word, not your needs. See, God isn't moved by your needs or anyone's needs. God isn't even moved by your tears, even though He does "feel" for you. The truth is, God is only moved by His Word. You've got to speak words of faith to God, not fear-filled pleas for help, if you ever want to see your prayers answered.

> *You've got to speak words of faith to God, not fear-filled pleas for help, if you ever want to see your prayers answered.*

Fear-Based Prayers

God will never answer fear-based prayers nor respond to fear-based praise. Many Christians decide they will pray and praise God because they need something to happen right away. They'll spend all day on their faces pleading with God, or singing and lifting their hands, trying to get Him to move quickly on their behalf. But what they don't realize is that any prayer or praise motivated by fear and not by faith is not received by God. When you send up fear-based prayers, you are actually pushing God farther and farther away from the equation, because just as Satan needs fear to operate in your life, God needs faith in order to move.

> *Any prayer or praise motivated by fear and not by faith is not received by God.*

Everything in the world system falls under two laws—the law of the Spirit of life in Christ Jesus or the law of sin and death (see Rom. 8:2). Love, healing, prosperity, deliverance, and faith are all found in the law of the Spirit of life in Christ Jesus, while sin, sickness, poverty, bondage, and fear are found under the law of sin and death. That means a prayer motivated by fear doesn't qualify to be answered because it originated from the wrong system.

Fear enters when you begin looking at your present situation and hearing the words of the enemy from TV, doctors, loved ones, and even your checkbook. Those words then create an atmosphere of doubt and unbelief. And once you start functioning in fear, you tie God's hands and cut off His access to your situation. Operating in fear will also hinder you from being able to receive and follow through on God's directions to you. Because of unbelief, when He tells you to do something, you won't obey because you doubt that He will follow through on His end of the deal.

Hebrews 11:6 says, "But without faith it is impossible to please him: for he that cometh to God must believe that he is, and that he is a rewarder of them that diligently seek him." You can't please God without faith. If doubt and unbelief are anywhere around, you negate your faith and sever your connection to God altogether. When fear is present, faith is not, and God can't do anything with a faithless prayer.

Believers need to understand that both fear and faith are spiritual connectors. Just like faith will connect you to the things you desire from the Word, fear will connect you to the things you fear the most. That's what happened to Job. Job was the greatest man in the whole East at one time, but he lost everything he had because of fear. Job 3:25 says, "For the thing which I greatly feared is come upon me, and that which I was afraid of is come unto me."

Job repeatedly offered sacrifices on behalf of his children because he feared his children may have sinned and offended God in some way. As a result of this demonstration of fear, he opened the door to the enemy to destroy everything he had. He lost all of his cattle and wealth, as well as his ten children. His fear put everything he had under the power of Satan, and negated the hedge of protection God had placed around him and his family (see Job 1:12). So out of fear, Job took what was meant to honor God and turned it into a fear-based ritual that connected him to what he feared the most, the death of his children.

So likewise, Christians must be careful that they don't take their prayers and praise, which are holy before the Lord, and transform them into powerless rituals. Don't say, "Well, I need to praise the Lord right now because they're about to put me out of my house," or tell your whole family to pray harder than they've ever prayed before so the "snatch man" doesn't come and repossess your car.

When you do that, you aren't praying or praising Him out of a heart of faith; you're doing it because you're desperate and scared. That's all fear-based, and God won't receive any of it. You are carrying out the form of prayer, but you lack the power of the Word of God to back it up. It doesn't matter how loud you scream, how long you pace the floor, or how hard you rock back and forth; if your prayers aren't Word-based, they won't go any higher than the ceiling.

It doesn't matter how loud you scream, how long you pace the floor, or how hard you rock back and forth; if your prayers aren't Word-based, they won't go any higher than the ceiling.

Please understand, it is the Word that fuels your prayers and gets God to respond, not your needs or begging and pleading. You don't pray to get God's attention or to try to get Him to do something, because He's already done all He's ever going to do. Hebrews 4:3 says, "For we which have believed do enter into rest, as he said, As I have sworn in my wrath, if they shall enter into my rest: although the works were finished from the foundation of the world."

God has already healed, prospered, delivered, and set you free, so now all you have to do is rest in His promises. Your stance as a believer is to stand on the promises you find in the Word. See, prayer is communication with God, believing and receiving what He has already given to us in Jesus. So getting your prayers answered is really on you. Everything that He's done is going to be based on your receiving and your believing what He has already said in His Word.

Prayer is saying to God what God has already said in His Word, and it is based on your having faith in the Word that God has already given to you. If you want results, your prayers must consist of releasing your faith in some specific area of God's Word, because the prayer system without the Word won't work. Otherwise you have simply had a kind of therapy session with God that made you feel a little better for the moment. If anything happens, it's because of the intercession of someone else on your behalf or it's because of the grace of God.

Fear-based prayers are the result of people who don't understand the true nature of God or His Word. God is not some tyrant or slave master. He's a loving Father who wants only the best for you. He desires more than anything to see His people prospering and having sweatless victory, but He has also set a system in place that He will not trespass. And since God won't change, it is up to us to learn the laws that govern this life and submit to them in order to be successful.

We have to open up our Bibles and find out what God has to say about our individual situations and then meditate on those Scriptures until they fill our hearts to overflowing. For example, if you have a terminal disease, meditate on Psalm 103:3–4, which says: "Who forgiveth all thine iniquities; who healeth all thy diseases; Who redeemeth thy life from destruction; who crowneth thee with loving kindness and tender mercies," until it becomes more real to you than that disease that's attacking your physical body. When your heart is full of the Word, your prayers will be fervent and produce the healing you desire, as opposed to making desperate pleas to God for the answers you hope for. Get your focus on Jesus!!

We have to open up our Bibles and find out what God has to say about our individual situations and then meditate on those Scriptures until they fill our hearts to overflowing.

God is not trying to make it hard for you to get your prayers answered; He understands and cares about everything you are going through. "For we have not an high priest which cannot be touched with the feeling of our infirmities; but was in all points tempted like as *we are*, yet without sin. Let us therefore come boldly unto the throne of grace, that we may obtain mercy, and find grace to help in time of need" (Heb. 4:15–16). He is full of compassion for you. He just wants you to come boldly to Him, believing that His Word already entitles you to total life prosperity.

God is not trying to make it hard for you to get your prayers answered; He understands and cares about everything you are going through.

Confidence in God

The key to answered prayer is your level of confidence in God, His Word, and His ability to bring it to pass. You'll find that the Word is always the common denominator in the prayer system. First John 5:14–15 says:

> *And this is the confidence (the assurance, the privilege of boldness) which we have in Him: [we are sure] that if we ask anything (make any request) according to His will (in agreement with His own plan), He listens to and hears us. And if (since) we [positively] know that He listens to us in whatever we ask, we also know [with settled and absolute knowledge] that we have [granted us as our present possessions] the request made of him.* (AMP)

When you pray according to the Word, you know God hears your requests. And if He hears you, then you know whatever you requested is your present possession, so it's a settled issue. No wavering back and forth. You must believe you've received your request the very moment you pray. "Therefore I say unto you, What things soever ye desire, when ye pray, believe that ye receive them, and ye shall have them" (Mark 11:24). The Amplified Bible says, "Whatever you ask for in prayer, believe (trust and be

confident) that it is granted to you, and you will [get it]." The key
to your confidence is your understanding of God's Word. When
you get on your face and you pray those Scriptures, it should be
settled then and there.

> *The key to your confidence is your understanding*
> *of God's Word. When you get on your face and*
> *you pray those Scriptures, it should be settled then*
> *and there.*

You must do whatever it takes to build your confidence. If you
have to take the Word of God concerning your finances, health,
or family into prayer with you, then do it. Just don't come out
of that prayer time and let your confidence wane. If you get off
your knees and somebody says, "Well, is it all right?" and you say,
"I don't know, we'll see," then you didn't believe you received it
when you prayed. When you believe you receive, you come out of
your prayer time saying, "Yeah, I got it!" And then from that point
on your response should be, "Amen, Lord. I believe I received that
when I prayed."

Plastic Prayers

Another way to make sure you get your prayers answered is to
pray to the Father in the name of Jesus. Many Christians still pray
to their Heavenly Father for "Christ's sake," which doesn't line up
with the Word. As a result, they are still praying religious "plastic"
prayers that don't connect with God.

That kind of prayer won't get results. Jesus said, "And in that day
ye shall ask me nothing. Verily, verily, I say unto you, Whatsoever

ye shall ask the Father in my name, he will give it you" (John 16:23). In this passage, Jesus clearly spells out the formula for successful prayer. Ask the Father in the name of Jesus, and the Father will give you whatsoever you ask—that lines up with the Word of God. As long as what you are praying is in the will of God, and you can find it in the Word, it's yours. That's why it's so important to study the Word of God and to learn exactly what you have a right to so that you can get results when you pray.

Ask the Father in the name of Jesus, and the Father will give you whatsoever you ask—that lines up with the Word of God.

Jesus felt that men "ought always to pray and not to turn coward (faint, lose heart, and give up)" (Luke 18:1 AMP). That means that after you have found the Scriptures that pertain to your situation, meditated on them until they filled your heart, and thanked the Father for them in Jesus' name, you are to stand on the promise until manifestation comes.

Don't let your present circumstances, discouraging words from others, or the lies of the devil move you off your stance of faith. You must be like the Apostle Paul and resolve to keep standing until you get what you are standing for (see Eph. 6:13–14). Let the Word of God anchor your soul and enable you to quench all the fiery darts of the devil. This strong stance in the Word will run fear clear out of your way, enabling you to stand strong in faith and be assured that your prayers will be answered speedily!

Let no man say when he is tempted, I am tempted
of God: for God cannot be tempted with evil,
neither tempteth he any man; But every man is
tempted, when he is drawn away of his own lust,
and enticed. Then when lust hath conceived, it
bringeth forth sin; and sin, when it is finished,
bringeth forth death.

JAMES 1:13–15

And Jesus answered and said unto him,
Get thee behind me, Satan: for it is written,
Thou shalt worship the Lord thy God, and him
only shalt thou serve.

LUKE 4:8

Keep thy heart with all diligence; for out of it *are*
the issues of life.

PROVERBS 4:23

REASON #3: RELIGION SAYS, "THE DEVIL MADE ME DO IT"

I know you've been there before. You miss the mark, and instead of owning up to the role you played in the situation, you hear the words *the devil made me do it* falling from your lips. That sin, if not dealt with, will develop into a habit that is hard to break. In a situation like this, it is often easier to blame the devil for why you did what you did because it takes the pressure and responsibility off you to make the necessary adjustments. The devil, however, is not your problem. I've often said that the real enemy in your life is actually "inner me," not Satan. An understanding of how sin unfolds in your life is necessary to put the brakes on lasciviousness.

Let me be clear—God is not the tempter—Satan is. But in the final analysis, the Bible doesn't say that the devil is responsible for making you sin. Religion may promote a different idea, but it's critical to stay with what the Word says on this subject, not tradition.

James 1:13–15 says, "Let no man say when he is tempted, I am tempted of God: for God cannot be tempted with evil, neither tempteth he any man: but every man is tempted, when he is drawn away of his own lust, and enticed. Then when lust hath conceived, it bringeth forth sin: and sin, when it is finished, bringeth forth death."

There are two key points to note in these Scriptures:

First, God does not tempt you to sin. I've heard people make Him out to be the bad guy, or they say that He will tempt you to see what you'll do in a certain situation, but that's simply not His M.O. While God may *allow* you to go through some things to try your faith, He is not the one bringing temptation to your doorstep. He is love, and Love wouldn't do that to His children.

> *While God may* **allow** *you to go through some things to try your faith, He is not the one bringing temptation to your doorstep.*

Second, the Bible says that a person is tempted when he or she is drawn away by his or her own lust. That means Satan uses the lust that is already in you by connecting it with his "bait." For example, if you constantly feed sexually charged images and words to your spirit through your eyes and ears, a seed of lust will be planted in your spirit. As you continue meditating on those things, that seed will begin to take root in your heart and eventually become a reality in your life.

I used to have difficulty resisting the temptation to eat apple pie. I *love* apple pie, and before I got control over the desire to eat it, I could devour a whole pie in one sitting. That was a real temptation for me. My grandmother used to stock her refrigerator with pie just for me, and I got used to satisfying my sweet tooth as I grew older. The seed was already in me, so I would fall every time. That seed was producing bad fruit in my life—my waistline was rapidly expanding, and I was dumping a lot of sugar in my system. I had to put the brakes on before my health started deteriorating. By renewing my mind in the area of taking care of my physical body, I was able to slow that desire down. Now I don't have to eat a whole pie in order to satisfy that craving. Thank God for His Grace!

Interestingly enough, the devil didn't make me eat those pies. He didn't put a gun to my head and force me to drive to the store and buy all the Little Debbie pies on the shelf. I made that decision on my own, because I had been meditating on his suggestions.

Satan is watching you to see how you respond in situations like this. Your challenge may not be with apple pies, but whatever area it is, he will try to capitalize on it. You have to know how to play the game in order to win.

When he sees the fruit of what you have been meditating on manifest in the natural realm, all he has to do is send something or someone to trigger you to act on the predominant seed in your spirit. So when the cute little secretary walks by and propositions you for sex, you'll be less likely to respond according to the Word of God. The problem wasn't the devil, but the lust that you had allowed to be deposited in your heart. You thought about it, talked about it, and acted out on it, plain and simple.

Verse 15 says that lust gives birth to sin. You see, Satan isn't so much concerned with getting you to sin, as much as he is with getting *you* to plant lust in your spirit. Because of the way the system is set up, he knows that if he can just get that lust in you, sin is inevitable. Lust *will* cause you to sin, and once you sin, you are on the pathway to death (see Rom. 6:23).

You most likely have never heard the sin process broken down this way before, but you're seeing it straight from the Word of God, which takes a lot of the responsibility off Satan and puts it on you. The real question is not why the devil keeps causing you to sin, but what are you giving him to work with?

> *The real question is not why the devil keeps causing you to sin, but what are you giving him to work with?*

No More Excuses

I'm tired of religion making excuses for people's failures and inadequacies. The biggest way to keep them from getting free from Satan's clutches is to get them to focus their attention on the wrong things. The devil is a master deceiver. He would love for you to focus all of your attention on him. He wants to take your mind off how you can take control over your own life. Instead of looking to Jesus for the way out, religion just covers up the truth.

Matthew 7:18 says that a good tree can't bring forth bad fruit and that a bad tree can't produce good fruit. That's because the condition of the roots of those trees determines the type of fruit they bring forth. I'm concerned with getting to the root issues of life. If I can get you to locate the root to why you do what you do, the *fruit* of your life will begin to change.

So let's take a look at the reasons why you are where you are. Very simply, it is your mind-set. The mind is the arena of faith and the battleground where Satan will wage war against you. It is also the control center for your life. Though your spirit was reborn when you accepted Jesus as your Lord and personal Savior, your mind didn't get saved! Here again, the responsibility is yours.

It is up to you to get in the Word of God and let it change your thinking.

Romans 12:1–2 says:

> *I beseech you therefore, brethren, by the mercies of God, that ye present your bodies a living sacrifice, holy, acceptable unto God, which is your reasonable service. And be not conformed to this world: but be ye transformed by the renewing of your mind, that ye may prove what is that good, and acceptable, and perfect, will of God.*

Here again, the responsibility is yours. It is up to you to get in the Word of God and let it change your thinking.

Quite simply, the results you're seeing in your life are the result of your mind-set. Whatever you set your mind on is what will become a reality for you. That's why the Apostle Paul admonishes believers to actively renew their minds. This is not a one-time event but an ongoing process that requires diligent meditation on the Word of God. It's the only way to purge your thinking of its old patterns. Someone may have told you not to spend *too* much time studying the Bible because it'll do something to your mind. Well, I want that Word to change my mind about things; I think of it as spiritual "brainwashing."

Washing bad thought patterns out of your mind with the Word is the best thing you can do for yourself. Proverbs 4:23 lets you know that the issues of your life flow out of what is in your heart. Your soul and spirit are connected, and this Scripture also refers to the soulish realm, or your mind, will, and emotions. It says,

"Keep thy heart with all diligence; for out of it are the issues of life." Your mind helps to set the course of your life.

Proverbs 23:7 also says, "For as he thinketh in his heart, so is he." What you think about on a constant basis forms the foundation of your life. If you meditate on worldly ideals and behavior, your actions will line up with those ideas. If you meditate on the Word of God, your life will be a reflection of that Word, and you will bring glory to the Father. Remember, the devil can't *make* you do anything. He can only *suggest* that you go in a certain direction. It is up to you whether or not you'll follow his leads.

> *If you meditate on worldly ideals and behavior, your actions will line up with those ideas. If you meditate on the Word of God, your life will be a reflection of that Word, and you will bring glory to the Father.*

The root of your behavior may be something you experienced in childhood, or even a value system that was imparted to you by your parents, friends, or church. If it doesn't line up with the Word, it needs to be removed.

Hebrews 4:12 says, "For the word of God is quick, and powerful, and sharper than any twoedged sword, piercing even to the dividing asunder of soul and spirit, and of the joints and marrow, and is a discerner of the thoughts and intents of the heart." The Word is stronger than any seed that may have been planted in you from childhood or anywhere else. Once you've located the roots to why you do what you do, allow the sword of the Spirit to cut them out so that you can begin to grow fruit that is pleasing to God.

Live Righteously

One of the fundamental keys to completely avoiding "the devil made me do it" syndrome is an understanding of who you are as the righteousness of God. Believers shouldn't be looking for a way to sin, but rather a way out of it. When you understand your righteousness, the tendency to follow the devil's plan for you is less likely. You don't have to yield to his attempts to lure you out of the will of God.

Believers shouldn't be looking for a way to sin,
but rather a way out of it.

When you were unsaved, you were under Satan's jurisdiction; you really had no choice but to sin because your spirit was connected to him. But since you've come out of darkness into the marvelous light of Jesus Christ, you've been set free from that mess. Romans 6:18 says of believers, "Being then made free from sin, ye became the servants of righteousness." One of Satan's biggest deceptions is to try to convince you that you're still subject to his authority, even though you've been born again. He wants you to think that when you miss the mark, God doesn't love you anymore. The most effective way to influence you to believe this lie is by keeping your mind bound in sin-consciousness.

Actually, religion is good at helping people hold on to their old sin tags. It preaches sin more than it does righteousness and focuses on beating people over their heads with a bunch of rules on what *not* to do instead of teaching them what *to* do. I believe that by focusing on the "do's" of the Bible, you'll gradually move away from all the "don'ts." You'll want to do right because

God says it's right and you love Him too much not to obey His commandments.

Righteousness has nothing to do with how well you perform in church, how many outreach ministries you are part of, or whether or not you operate in the gifts of the Spirit. Rather, it is all about what Jesus did for you on the cross. He died so that you could be *made* righteous. This miracle happened instantaneously when you confessed Him as Lord and Savior. There's nothing you can or can't do to earn or lose this gift. God sees you through a new set of lenses—Jesus lenses. He doesn't view your sin the way you do.

Righteousness grants you access to every promise and provision God has made in His Word. From healing and deliverance, to household salvation and debt cancellation, it's all yours if you lay hold of it by faith.

Let's say you miss the mark or sin by doing something that goes against the Word of God. As the righteousness of God, your responsibility is to take that thing before God and exchange it for His cleansing and forgiveness. Know your rights! Don't wallow around in self-pity and get into guilt and condemnation about it. The devil would love for you to do that. No, just get up, brush yourself off, and keep moving in the things of God.

Now, I'm not suggesting that you use your righteousness as an excuse to keep sinning. That's trying to take advantage of God, and He won't be mocked (see Gal. 6:7). If you sow to your flesh, you'll reap a fleshly, carnal harvest that you don't want, whether you are born again or not. I'm simply saying that when you do miss it, exercise your righteousness and move on.

Righteousness even goes a step farther. At some point, you have to reach the level where you don't have to keep exercising your righteousness because sin is ruling your life. All of us miss it at times, but when you find yourself in lasciviousness in a particular area, it's time for some serious mind renewal.

God wants you to get to the point where you realize that you don't *have* to sin if you don't want to. Righteousness should be a consciousness that restrains you from doing things contrary to the Word in the first place.

> *God wants you to get to the point where you realize that you don't **have** to sin if you don't want to.*

I can hear someone saying, *I hear what you're saying, Brother Dollar, but I just don't think it's possible not to sin.* I'm here to tell you that the grace of God will teach you to live a godly, righteous life (Titus 2:11, 12). Trust Jesus!!

Child of God, righteousness is right standing with God. Essentially, it is a stance that is aligned with Him. In other words, you're not the same person you used to be. The sin that dominated your mind and body has been disconnected from you. Meditating in the reality of your righteousness will change your mind and give you a revelation of your true identity as a born-again child of God.

When you understand your relationship with God, there is nothing the enemy can do to entice you to go back to that old way of life. He can throw suggestions and temptations at you all day, but he'll end up bumping into your righteousness every time. After a while, he'll find someone else to harass. It's the guy who knows he's righteous who'll be able to successfully defeat the enemy.

Righteousness is an integral part of the believer's existence. It is even listed as part of the armor of God. No soldier would go into battle without being adequately suited up with the proper protective gear. Well, the righteousness of God is part of your "spiritual battle uniform" that you can't afford to leave at home.

Ephesians 6:11–14 says this:

> *Put on the whole armor of God, that ye may be able to stand*
> *against the wiles of the devil. For we wrestle not against flesh*
> *and blood, but against principalities, against powers, against*
> *the rulers of the darkness of this world, against spiritual wick-*
> *edness in high places. Wherefore take unto you the whole*
> *armour of God, that ye may be able to withstand in the evil*
> *day, and having done all to stand. Stand therefore, having*
> *your loins girt about with truth, and having on the breast-*
> *plate of righteousness.*

Righteousness is a vital part of your spiritual covering because
it protects your position in God. What I mean is that everything
you do for the kingdom of God has to be covered by your being
in right standing with Him, or else it is worthless. When you
pray, you have to know that you have a right to get your prayers
answered. When you sow a financial seed, your confidence in
your righteousness through the blood of Jesus assures you that
harvest time is right around the corner.

Everything you do for the kingdom of God has to be
covered by your being in right standing with Him,
or else it is worthless.

Notice that the word *righteousness* is used to describe your spiritual "breastplate." This part of your armor covers and protects
your heart, or your spirit man. When you don't know who you
are in Christ (as the righteousness of God), you'll become easy
prey for the kingdom of darkness. You won't have confidence
in your prayers being answered, or even the fact that God loves

you. When your breastplate is out of place, you'll do a lot of good works to get God's attention, and you'll fall for every trick of the enemy in the process.

Your right standing with God is not something you can gauge by your feelings. There will be times when you don't *feel* righteous at all, particularly if you've missed it. But God doesn't operate in the realm of feelings. He operates in the realm of faith, and righteousness is something you have to lay hold of by faith (see Rom. 9:30). That means that no matter what is going on in your life, no matter what you've done or haven't done, and no matter what anyone tries to tell you, you know that you are rightly related to God because Jesus is your Lord. Knowing this enables you to stand in the midst of life's trials and tests with the courage and confidence that are necessary to be an overcoming Christian.

No matter what is going on in your life, no matter what you've done or haven't done, and no matter what anyone tries to tell you, you know that you are rightly related to God because Jesus is your Lord.

God has set a standard in place by which He wants you to live. It includes the abundant life full of blessings and prosperity. But a righteousness-consciousness is critical to tapping into it. You have complete control over the direction you want your life to take, and by reprogramming your mind with the Word, your course will be set.

It's time for you to step up and take responsibility for where you are. Know yourself, know your issues, and get in the Word of God to find out what the prescription is for whatever you're facing. Locate your areas of weakness and make a decision to dig up any bad seeds you've sown in your spirit by diligently applying the necessary Scriptures to those areas.

Remember, blaming the devil for your problems is just a religious way to avoid having the trust and faith to maintain a life of holiness. Making excuses won't solve anything; it will only keep you trapped in a cycle of continual sin. However, by allowing righteousness to reign in your life, you'll be equipped with the confidence to know that you can get out of Satan's sin traps, and stay out forever. You don't have to fall because you are more than a conqueror!

But now being made free from sin, and become servants to God, ye have your fruit unto holiness, and the end everlasting life, For the wages of sin *is* death; but the gift of God *is* eternal life through Jesus Christ our Lord.

ROMANS 6:22–23

I know thy works, that thou art neither cold nor hot; I would thou wert cold or hot. So then because thou art lukewarm, and neither cold nor hot, I will spue thee out of my mouth.

REVELATION 3:15–16

For ever, O Lord, thy word is settled in heaven.

PSALM 119:89

REASON #2: RELIGION BELIEVES IT'S OKAY TO SIN UNDER GRACE

Have you ever been to a church where the Word of grace was "watered down" in order to appease the people? In other words, the preacher danced around the key issues of what the congregation needed to know, just so he could avoid offending anyone. There are a lot of churches like this.

They don't explain what grace is and what grace is not. They fail to mention how grace completely transforms lives because they fear the message won't be accepted, or their membership will decrease. Instead of preaching the truth and letting people know about God's favor, they promote the idea that "God understands" and that as long as you are a "good" person, you can sin all you want and still experience the good life. This is simply another religious tactic of the enemy that is designed to keep people in bondage to the law of sin and death.

Politically or Scripturally Correct?

A lot of things are politically correct, but the question is, are they spiritual and scripturally correct? This has become a challenge in the Body of Christ. Many times, people are willing to compromise the truth of God's Word in order to pacify popular worldly mind-sets and ideals. For example, certain pastors may say that God loves you, and certainly He wouldn't expect you to be perfect; after all, you're human, right? But they omit preaching about grace, which is an important aspect of God's personality.

The obsession with political correctness in our culture and society is responsible for keeping people blinded from the truth they need to be set free from bondage. It masks the commandments of God with religious excuses that enable the people of God to continue in deception and sin. Even when you're born again and Jesus is living inside you, He understands that you're going to slip up sometimes and sin. But He doesn't want you to *stay* in sin.

> *Even when you're born again and Jesus is living inside you, He understands that you're going to slip up sometimes and sin. But He doesn't want you to* stay *in sin.*

Instead of trying to gloss over this issue with religious ideas, let's find out what the Bible has to say about it. Jude 1:3–4 says, "Dear friends, I wanted very much to write to you concerning the salvation we share. Instead, I must write to urge you to fight for the faith delivered once and for all to God's holy people. God-less people have slipped in among you. They turn the grace of our

God into unrestrained immorality and deny our only master and Lord, Jesus Christ. Judgment was passed against them a long time ago" (CEV).

Grace is not a license to keep sinning. This kind of thinking was a problem then, and it continues to be a problem today. If you continue in sin, you open the back door for Satan to wreak havoc in your life. Jesus dealt with sin on the cross of Calvary, but we must believe His sacrifice in order to be cleansed of our sin.

When we receive Jesus, grace empowers us and enables us to live for God and carry out His Word in our lives. God will never withdraw His love from you. However, sin has consequences that you don't want to deal with.

Being True from the Inside Out

Religion promotes condemnation and makes people feel as if they can't ever truly break out of those old mind-sets. Religion embraces the parts of the Word that feel good, but it doesn't focus on the source of all these blessings. Child of God, the source is Jesus, Who is grace—unearned, unmerited, undeserved favor from God—in human form.

> *Religion embraces the parts of the Word that feel good, but it doesn't focus on the source of all these blessings.*

Contrary to traditional religious concepts and teachings, holiness doesn't come from wearing long skirts and going without makeup. "We have been made holy by God's will through the offering of Jesus Christ's body once for all" (Hebrews 10:10 CEV). Accepting by faith Jesus' death and resurrection is what gives us our right standing with God, not our own deeds or actions.

Religion has turned holiness into an unattainable ideal that has to do with outer appearance, but that is far from the truth. Until grace arrived on the scene, the world was trapped in sin and death. What Jesus did for you and me on the cross was a game changer, and made victory and eternal life possible for everyone. When you accept and believe in the works of grace and the power they wield, holiness becomes completely attainable, and your outer appearance, conduct, and mind-set will begin to change.

Correcting False Teachings

Another misconception is that when you're living under grace, you'll always be the tail and not the head. Grace is not an excuse to settle for miserable circumstances. Life can throw some real curve balls, but when you feel like you're a victim of circumstances, grace strengthens you in the midst of your situation. Whether your lights have been turned off, your car's been repossessed, or you're about to be evicted, grace will give you what you need to improve the situation and ultimately succeed.

Life can throw some real curve balls, but when you feel like you're a victim of circumstances, grace strengthens you in the midst of your situation.

"For the law was given through Moses; grace and truth came through Jesus Christ" (John 1:17 NIV). During His earthly ministry, Jesus wasn't concerned about being politically correct at the expense of the truth. He called a spade a spade, and He didn't get along with the religious folks. Coming out of religion, which is based on works and rituals, and accepting what God's Word has for you, is a liberating experience. "Jesus said to the people who believed in him, 'You are truly my disciples if you remain faithful to my teachings. And you will know the truth, and the truth will set you free'" (John 8:31–32 NLT).

Trusting God and His Word positions you to receive the fullness of God's promises in every area of your life. You see, everything goes back to you having a genuine relationship with Him, and not how well you can look like a Christian in church. Following God's instructions to us is optional, because we are free moral agents. However, following His instructions to us is the key to living a successful life.

Religion requires us to perform work after work, but a grace-based relationship with God encourages us to rest in Him. Jesus said, "Come unto me, all ye that labour and are heavy laden, and I will give you rest" (Matt. 11:28). This is where some people get confused. As I mentioned in an earlier chapter, grace is not a license to be lazy and "resting in God" doesn't mean inactivity. What it does mean is that when we trust grace to work for us, in us, and through us, our determination and resolve to work harder than others with less effort to achieve vastly superior results comes from God.

When we trust grace to work for us, in us, and through us, our determination and resolve to work harder than others with less effort to achieve vastly superior results comes from God.

When you receive God's love for you, you'll turn away from the sins you used to enjoy because He loves you so much. With grace living in you, you won't *want* to sin anymore, because it just won't feel right. That's the power of the Holy Spirit working on you from the inside, and no amount of religious church doctrine can change you like that!

Meditating on God's Promises

I have a problem with the hymn "Gimme That Old Time Religion," something you've probably grown up hearing and sung many times in church. You see, some—though not all—traditional religions are in direct opposition to the teachings of Jesus, and the danger is that most people haven't given this much thought. They just mindlessly accept whatever the preacher throws at them from the pulpit, without questioning it. When I leave this earth and go to heaven, I want people to remember me for the relationship I had with Jesus, not how religious I was.

When I leave this earth and go to heaven, I want people to remember me for the relationship I had with Jesus, not how religious I was.

Religious teachings lean toward instilling fear and self-effort in us, and church leaders have used them for centuries to control the people and keep them in subjugation. They love to condemn, in order to keep folks in line. Compare this with what the Scriptures say and make your own decisions. "For God hath not given us the spirit of fear; but of power, and of love, and of a sound mind" (2 Tim. 1:7).

This freedom from fear is something you don't hear too much about, maybe because many don't even believe this promise themselves. It's available as part of a grace-based package of salvation, victory, and eternal life. If you believe, it automatically becomes available at no cost to you, although Jesus paid the ultimate price on the cross for this freedom. Which brings me to another point—grace is not cheap.

No doubt you hear the popular slogan "Freedom is not free" every Memorial Day and Veterans Day, but the biblical meaning of this phrase goes even deeper than its earthly meaning. The freedom that grace brings you includes freedom from fear, from death, from failure, from lack and insufficiency, from poverty, from addictions, and from so many other evils that defeat the world. This free gift to you is something Jesus bought with His own blood, and when you believe in the power of what He did, you are made righteous and holy in God's eyes.

> *The freedom that grace brings you includes freedom from fear, from death, from failure, from lack and insufficiency, from poverty, from addictions, and from so many other evils that defeat the world.*

Too often, churchgoers get caught up with gossip and playing church roles, pretending to be outwardly religious. You've probably seen it in others' selfish or judgmental attitudes, and it happens when people lose sight of who they should focus on. This is not what God wants for His church. "If any man among you seem to be religious, and bridleth not his tongue, but deceiveth his own heart, this man's religion is vain" (James 1:26). Distractions like these are one of the tactics the devil uses to divide God's church, but grace brings everything back into perspective.

Grace, the "Real Deal"

The last point I want to make here is that grace comes from a God full of grace. The first thing that jumps out at me is how God sought out Mary, a young, unwed girl, to give birth to Jesus. God offers us His grace out of love for us, with no regard as to whether we're worthy of it or not. This girl was most likely a nobody in the world's eyes, but God sent an angel to deliver a different message. "And he came to her and said, Hail, O favored one [endued with grace]! The Lord is with you! Blessed (favored of God) are you before all other women! But when she saw him, she was greatly troubled and disturbed and confused at what he said and kept revolving in her mind what such a greeting might mean. And the angel said to her, Do not be afraid, Mary, for you have found grace (free, spontaneous, absolute favor and loving-kindness) with God" (Luke 1:28–30 AMP).

> *God offers us His grace out of love for us, with no regard as to whether we're worthy of it or not.*

Most likely, the religious leaders of the time never would have thought that God's favor would descend on someone with such a lowly social standing. To endue is to bestow or provide a gift, and in this case the gift was the Son of God Himself.

Now, if grace can seek out someone like Mary, who was invisible to the high church leaders, He can certainly find you. Religion will try and convince you that you're not worth God's favor, condemn you for all your past mistakes, and use scare tactics to keep you from realizing the love God has for you. But check out what the angel told Mary—not to fear.

Jesus, who is truth (see John 14:6), sees right though us, and He sees what's in our hearts. That's something empty religious practices could never do. Don't let religion blind you to the truth, and don't let it mislead you about the true nature of God. When you're not afraid to embrace His grace, He'll surely show up and abundantly bless your life.

> *Don't let religion blind you to the truth, and don't let it mislead you about the true nature of God. When you're not afraid to embrace His grace, He'll surely show up and abundantly bless your life.*

Then came to Jesus scribes and Pharisees, which were of Jerusalem, saying, Why do thy disciples transgress the tradition of the elders? For they wash not their hands when they eat bread. But he answered and said unto them, Why do ye also transgress the commandments of God by your tradition?

MATTHEW 15:1–3

And he said unto them, The Sabbath was made for man, and not man for the Sabbath: Therefore the Son of man is Lord also of the Sabbath.

MARK 2:27–28

For God so loved the world, that he gave his only begotten Son, that whosoever believeth in him should not perish, but have everlasting life.

JOHN 3:16

10

REASON #1: RELIGION ALLOWS PEOPLE TO BE SELFISH

There is a nasty monster on the loose that is blocking the power of God from operating through the Body of Christ as it should. You may think the culprit is the hard-to-deal-with usher who hassles you when you try to take your seat in church, or the co-worker who gets on your last nerve, but the problem is neither. The monster I am referring to is selfishness, and it's destroying the lives of believers. Religion has set the stage for selfishness to abound in the church, and it's time to deal with it and eradicate it so the Body of Christ can begin to walk in the "greater works" Jesus spoke about.

Know this: God is love. The very nature of our Father is love. He doesn't just have it; He *is* it. His love for you was demonstrated when He sent His Son, Jesus, to die for your sins (see John 3:16). I want to point out something very key in this Scripture. It says that He so loved the world that He *gave*. The number one characteristic of love is that it is always concerned with giving to others. It looks for new and creative ways to be a blessing at all times. Contrary to the world's view of love, which is demonstrated in popular songs and movies, it isn't a "mushy" warm and fuzzy feeling. Neither is it some kind of romantic sentiment. No, the God kind of love always has action to back it up. To say that you love someone but are unwilling to give of yourself for that person, according to the Word's standard, shows your lack of understanding where love is concerned.

> *Know this: God is love. The very nature of our Father is love. He doesn't just have it; He is it.*

Selfishness, on the other hand, takes from others. It isn't concerned with giving the advantage but rather taking advantage in whatever way it can. That explains why all sin is based in selfishness. No matter what area of the flesh you are dealing with, if you find yourself succumbing to it, you can be assured that selfishness is in operation.

Walls of Protection

Religion is a counterfeit form of Christianity. Instead of allowing love to flow to meet people's needs, it places walls around selfishness to protect it and keep it intact. For example, one erroneous religious belief is that doing a bunch of good works will make God love you more. Nothing could be farther from the truth. However, people who do a lot of good works in hopes of getting into God's good graces may actually be trying to protect feelings of inadequacy or low self-esteem. They may do things to try to impress others rather than out of love for people. What a selfish attitude!

It is an attitude that is concerned with how they appear to others rather than how to please God. It is a self-protective stance that attempts to use church service as a method of self-preservation.

Another selfish religious mind-set is one that believes that the devil makes us sin. Again, this attitude avoids taking responsibility for one's actions. It also can become an excuse for continuing to miss the mark. Blaming the devil for sinful behavior is actually an attempt to protect the sin in order to continue doing it. It becomes easy to continue indulging in that activity when the devil is used as a scapegoat all the time.

When people are selfish, they want to preserve where they are at that particular time. They don't want to take the risk of changing because they have grown comfortable in their way of life. Isn't that how religious people function? They don't want to change because they fear having to own up to their behavior.

Jesus told the Pharisees that their tradition made the Word of God have no effect (see Matt. 15:3–6). The religious leaders of His day had grown comfortable in their religion. It felt good for them to impose hundreds of laws on the people because it made them look as if they were ultra-spiritual, even though people were walking around poor, sick, and oppressed. When Jesus challenged their teachings, they couldn't handle it. He was trying to get them to change the way they thought about things so the spiritual needs of the people could be met. Their selfishness prevented them from doing that.

That's exactly what religion does. It protects selfishness at the expense of others. The people in the pews need the power of the Word to operate in their lives, not a religious display of form. Just as Jesus challenged the Pharisees, we need to challenge one another to break out of tradition and break into the truth of God's love for us.

*Just as Jesus challenged the Pharisees, we need
to challenge one another to break out of tradition
and break into the truth of God's love for us.*

Opposing Forces

If things aren't working for you, most likely the problem is a love issue. The bottom line is that you have to come away from constantly being concerned about yourself if you expect the Word of God to produce results. God is a giver, and as His children, we should get on the giving side of life as well. That is what walking in love is all about.

Selfishness is the opposite of love, just as fear is the opposite of faith. The two simply cannot coexist. Anytime selfishness is operating in your life, the law of sin and death is actively working to stop the harvest you are asking God to bring to you.

*Selfishness is the opposite of love, just as fear
is the opposite of faith. The two simply cannot
coexist.*

I want you to see something from the Scriptures that demonstrates how selfishness can block God from showing up in your life. Look at Mark 10:17–22:

*And when he was gone forth into the way, there came one
running, and kneeled to him, and asked him, Good Master,
what shall I do that I may inherit eternal life? And Jesus said*

unto him, Why callest thou me good? There is none good but one, that is, God. Thou knowest the commandments, Do not commit adultery, Do not kill, Do not steal, Do not bear false witness, Defraud not, Honour thy father and mother. And he answered and said unto him, Master, all these have I observed from my youth. Then Jesus beholding him loved him, and said unto him, One thing thou lackest: go thy way, sell whatsoever thou hast, and give to the poor, and thou shalt have treasure in heaven: and come, take up the cross and follow me. And he was sad at that saying, and went away grieved: for he had great possessions.

This young man needed Jesus' ministry. Obviously, he was going through some things because he asked Jesus what the key to eternal life was. He stated that he knew the Law, the commandments of God. And yet he had no clue as to how to inherit the good life. That sounds like a lot of church folk I know. They know the principles and the methods, but when it comes to really tapping into the abundant, Zoë life, they have no clue. Religion has prevented them from getting understanding.

Jesus told this young man that although he knew the last six commandments, all of which dealt with loving others, when it came to loving God with all of his heart, soul, mind, strength, and possessions, he fell short. Most likely this young man followed the traditions of his religion, yet he was selfish when it came to his personal belongings. He was not willing to let go of his material wealth and follow Jesus. Consequently, his unwillingness to step out of selfishness and reach out to others caused him to miss out on being a part of the greatest ministry on earth. His selfishness was protected by his religion, and he went away more depressed than he was when he came to Jesus.

What have you missed out on because you insisted on

protecting selfishness in your life? Every time God presents you with an opportunity to come out of that way of thinking, a blessing awaits you on the other side of your obedience. Unlike love, selfishness tries to convince you that by obeying God and walking in love, you somehow miss out on something. That's just a trick of the enemy. The truth is that when you don't come out of your comfort zone, you miss out on the blessings of God.

What have you missed out on because you insisted on protecting selfishness in your life?

The Great Commandment

In Matthew 22:37–40, Jesus gives the love laws. The first and great commandment is to love the Lord your God with all of your heart, soul, mind, and strength. He says that the second great commandment, which is just as weighty as the first, is to love your neighbor as yourself. To violate these commandments puts you in a dangerous position. Under the covenant of grace, we love as God has loved us.

Staying in the "circle of love" places you in God's protection. In this circle are the blessings of God, which include prosperity, healing, deliverance, and the abundant life. Every promise God has made to you can be found within the confines of the love circle, because He is love!

Outside that circle exists the law of sin and death. How does Satan get you out of the protection of God? He often sends people and situations your way to offend you, or he gets you to operate in selfishness in any capacity. When you get off into this unprotected territory, you are open to his attacks. Because you are on his turf, he has every right to successfully deter you from the will of God for your life. His fiery darts can penetrate your spirit when you step out of love.

Staying "in the circle" is critical to the quality of life you will lead as a believer; selfish people are never successful. Though they may look like they are on the outside, their souls are sick because God created us to give of ourselves to others so that they may prosper. Selfish people withhold certain areas of their lives from God. As a result, they do not experience the total life prosperity that is described in 3 John 1:2.

Can you see why Jesus said that loving God and your neighbor are the two most important laws? As God's children, we are to imitate Him (see Eph. 5:1–2), which means loving others as Christ loved us. Living this way is like having an automatic protection plan in place every single day. You don't have to worry about death, sickness, poverty, and bondage attaching themselves to you when you are actively keeping the commandments and guarding against selfishness.

As God's children, we are to imitate Him, which means loving others as Christ loved us.

Perfecting the Love of God

Many times, as Christians, we hear about walking in love, but we really don't understand the nuts and bolts of how to have a good "love life" with God and others. Like everything in the kingdom of God, there is a process involved in perfecting the love of God. Just as mind renewal is a daily experience and not a one-time event, so is perfecting the love of God in your life. It is going to take diligence, effort, and most important, a quality decision to live this type of lifestyle.

The sin question really has a simple answer—get rid of selfishness and perfect the love of God. You see, all sin is selfish. From fornication and adultery to lust and hatred, these are the works of a carnal mind-set that is primarily concerned with fulfilling its own selfish desires. A person who commits fornication is not thinking about the well-being of the person with whom he or she is having sex. He or she isn't considering the serious spiritual and physical ramifications of that activity.

Similarly, people who have no temperance where eating is concerned will succumb to a spirit of gluttony. Instead of eating to sustain their physical bodies and keep them in optimum health, the focus is on satisfying a selfish, greedy desire. These people aren't concerned about the effects that their actions will have on their health. God didn't create the body to be abused through any type of lustful activity. Your body is the temple of the Holy Spirit, and should be regarded as such. To violate your body is to demonstrate your selfishness and lack of regard for God and those to whom He has ordained you to be a blessing.

The first step to perfecting the love of God is to make a quality decision. You have to settle the issue forever: as a child of God, you *are* going to walk in love, no matter what. As soon as you do that, be aware that Satan is going to throw everything he can at you to get you to move off your stance of love. But don't be discouraged. Your big brother, Jesus, went through the same test, and passed! You can pass, too.

*You have to settle the issue forever: as a child of God, you **are** going to walk in love, no matter what.*

I look at the work of the flesh listed in Galatians 5:19–21 as the works of selfishness. Without selfishness in operation, these activities have nothing to stand on. Adultery, fornication, uncleanness, lasciviousness, idolatry, witchcraft, hatred, variance, emulations, wrath, strife, seditions, heresies, envy, murder, drunkenness, and wild partying are all the results of a selfish, carnal mind-set. You cut yourself off from the blessings of God when you do these things.

On the flip side of that coin are the fruits of the Spirit, headed up by the love of God. The components of His love include joy, peace, long-suffering, gentleness, goodness, faith, meekness, and temperance. By cultivating these facets of love, you counteract the fruit of the carnal mind and inherit God's promises.

I suggest that you begin practicing the love of God in the seemingly small areas. For example, you may be stuck in bumper-to-bumper traffic and want to blow your top. But don't do that! Look at it as an opportunity to develop an aspect of the fruit of the Spirit. Let the confession of your mouth lead your mind and actions to line up with God's love. Instead of cussing out the driver in front of you or blowing your horn, declare that you'll use the situation to walk in love. Pop a teaching tape in the CD player, or put some praise music on. As you start thanking and praising God for something good He's done for you, you'll find your frustration melting away. Or pray in the Spirit, which also helps to keep you in the love circle (Jude 1:20–21).

Another way to perfect God's love is to actively work on loving your enemies every day. That's right, love your enemies! There may be people whom you don't see every day who have offended or hurt you in some way. Or there may be someone you know who doesn't like you, with whom you really don't have too much communication. Just because you don't have regular verbal exchanges with someone doesn't mean you are off the hook. This is an opportunity for you to practice loving him or her in the spirit, by praying for and confessing the Word over his or her life.

Now I know that's hard on your flesh! Who wants to pray for and declare blessings over someone who has offended or hurt you? How you feel doesn't really amount to a hill of beans. What matters most is what God has said, and He has commanded us to love our neighbors.

At first it will be challenging to pray for the difficult people in your life. But when you set your love thermometer at a specific setting and refuse to let it waver, it will get easier to bless those who have cursed you or used you. This is the heart of walking in love—loving the unlovable. That's what Jesus did. He prayed for the very people who were crucifying Him, while He was dying on the cross! I don't know anyone who has had to endure that kind of suffering, and yet Jesus was determined not to violate the commandments of His Father. Because He loved God, He obeyed that second commandment. We are commissioned to do the same.

> *This is the heart of walking in love—loving the unlovable. That's what Jesus did.*

If you know that you've been walking in selfishness, don't get into condemnation about it. God is faithful and just to forgive you of sin and cleanse you of all unrighteousness (1 John 1:9). Make a decision to turn away from a selfish lifestyle and make the love of God your way of life. Practice daily on people and situations until the love lifestyle comes naturally to you. Be encouraged that the Holy Spirit will strengthen you when you are weak and help you to stay on course.

Don't let religion keep you in a position of defeat. God's power can't flow through people who are trapped in this way of thinking. The devil would love for you to remain locked into traditional beliefs that actually keep you in bondage. But when you get a revelation of God's love for you, you'll see that being a Christian is more than doing all the "churchy" things. It is about a personal love relationship with the Father and Jesus.

> *Being a Christian is more than doing all the "churchy" things. It is about a personal love relationship with the Father and Jesus.*

When you deal with the excuses that are keeping you bound, you can start to see victory. Selfishness has to be dealt with in order to experience all that God has for you. He is a loving God, and He wants us to be His children of love. Tradition and religion will leave you in lack because the love of God isn't present there. I invite you to come into the knowledge of this love and experience all that God has for you.

ABOUT THE AUTHOR

Dr. Creflo Dollar is the founder and senior pastor of World Changers Church International (WCCI) in College Park, Georgia; World Changers Church—New York; and satellite churches such as World Changers Church—Houston, Los Angeles, and Norcross. His award-winning *Changing Your World* broadcast reaches nearly one billion homes around the world. Dr. Dollar is the publisher of *Change*, an online magazine featuring inspiring, challenging, and life-changing articles that deal with everyday life issues, and *The Max*, a resource newsletter for ministry leaders. A much-sought-after conference speaker, Dr. Dollar has books, CDs, audiotapes, and videotapes in worldwide distribution. He is the author of *The Holy Spirit, Your Financial Advisor, 8 Steps to Create the Life You Want, Winning in Troubled Times*, and *Real Manhood*. He and his wife, Taffi, have five children and live in Atlanta, Georgia. You can visit Creflo Dollar Ministries at CrefloDollarMinistries.org.